The big story of the Bible

An easy read journey
through God's special book

by Jo Acharya

Valley of Springs
PUBLISHING

ISBN 978-1-7399273-3-2 spiralbound
ISBN 978-1-7399273-4-9 paperback

What other people are saying about 'The Big Story of the Bible'

Contents

You can read this page any time!

About this book

My name is Jo and I wrote this book. It is for everyone who wants to know more about the Bible.

This book has easy words and helpful pictures. I wrote it this way to help people who find reading hard.

anyone *finds*

I hope this book will help you see how the Bible fits together into one big story. And I hope it will help you get to know God better.

The Bible is full of stories. An old woman has an impossible baby. A man gets swallowed by a whale. A brave queen saves her people.

But the Bible is also one big story. This is God's story. It tells us how the world got broken, and God's plan to fix it. And it is the story of God's friendship with people like you and me.

This book is a journey through the Bible. We will meet lots of different people who trusted God. We will uncover God's plan to fix the world. And we will learn how we can be part of God's story too.

How to read this book

You can read this book as fast or slow as you like. You do not have to read a whole chapter. You can read just one page at a time.

If you want to understand the big story of the Bible, it is a good idea to read from the start to the end.

But you can also look up any part of the story at any time.

→ Main chapters

The main chapters take you through the big story of the Bible.

The start of each chapter tells you who this part of the story is about, and where you can find it in the Bible.

Then there is a quick look at what you are about to learn.

The rest of the chapter takes you through one part of the story.

There is one main Bible verse and some questions and prayers. At the end, you learn how this chapter fits into the big story.

→ Zoom in chapters

The zoom in chapters tell you more about some important things in the story. They help you understand what the big story of the Bible means.

Some of the zoom in chapters might take a bit longer to understand. You can read them as you go along, or you can come back to them later.

→ Indexes and word meanings

If you want to look up a person or book of the Bible, the indexes at the back of the book will help you find the right page.

There are some word meanings at the end of the book too. They will help you understand new words.

→ Coloured writing

As you go along, you will see some writing in different colours.

Bible verses in pink like this (Genesis chapter 2 verses 4-25) tell you where in the Bible you can find out more.

Page numbers in pink like this (Page 72) tell you where in this book you can find out more.

Words in dark blue are words from the Bible.

If you need help

The Bible is a big book. It was written long ago, when life was very different. The Bible also teaches us new things. It takes time to understand these things.

So do not worry if you do not understand everything in this book to start with. You do not need to understand everything to be friends with God.

Even people who have trusted God for a long time are still learning more about him!

It is a good idea to talk to another Christian about what you are learning. They can help you if you have questions or want to know more. If you like, you can ask them to read the book with you.

You can ask God for help too. God wants to help you get to know him better.

This does not mean you will understand everything. But God will help you understand the most important things.

God makes the world

God made the world. He made people. Then he rested.

Genesis chapters 1-2

Adam
Eve

 **Quick look**

Looks like a magician! Merlin maybe!

God made the world and everything in it.

Everything God made was good.

God made people too. He loves us very much.

God gave his people a garden to live in.

A good world

At the start, there was nothing. Then God made everything.

God made the sun, moon and stars. He made the world. He made water and land. He made the fish, birds and animals.

plants + trees?

God made people too. He made us to be like him. He made us to be friends with him.

God loves people very much.

 **What are some good things in the world?**

do you expect people to write here? If so a pencil icon might make that clearer, & a bigger/extended box?

12

The first people

(Genesis chapter 2 verses 4-25)

God took some dust from the ground. He made a man out of the dust. Then God breathed into the man's nose. The man came to life. God called the man Adam.

Then God said **"It is not good for the man to be alone."** (Genesis chapter 2 verse 18, ERV) God wanted to make more people. He wanted people to love and help each other.

So God made Adam fall asleep. He took a bone from Adam's body. He made a woman out of the bone.

Adam woke up and saw the woman. He knew she was the friend he needed. Adam was very happy. He called the woman Eve.

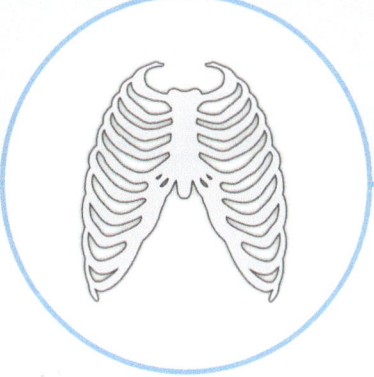

Adam needed other people. I need other people too.

Everyone needs to be loved. And everyone needs help sometimes. We all need good friends.

Think about the people who love and help you. Thank God for each of them.

God rests

Everything God made was very good. There was nothing bad in the world.

> God looked at everything he had made. And he saw that everything was very good.
>
> (Genesis chapter 1 verse 31, ERV)

God was very happy with the world he had made. He gave Adam and Eve a beautiful garden to live in.

God told Adam and Eve to have children and look after the world.

 How can you help to look after the world?

God made me the person I am. He decided what I would be like and what I would be good at.

God made me special. No one else is just like me!

Think of some good things about you. Thank God for making you the person you are.

The big story...

When God made the world, everything was good. There was no pain or sadness.

People were friends with God and with each other. That is the way God wants it to be.

People turned away from God. They did bad things. This broke the world.

Genesis chapters 3-11

Adam
Eve
Noah

 Quick look

God told people the best way to live.

But people turned away from God. They did what God said not to do.

People could not stop doing bad things. Everything was going wrong.

A lying snake

There was a tree in the middle of the garden. God gave Adam and Eve one rule. He told them not to eat any fruit from this tree.

This fruit would make Adam and Eve know what was good and what was bad. God said if they ate it they would die.

But a snake told lies to Adam and Eve. The snake said God was not good. The snake said the fruit would make them as clever as God. It said they would not really die if they ate it.

Adam and Eve believed the snake. They ate the fruit.

God was angry. His people did not trust him. They did what he had told them not to do. So he sent them out of the garden.

 Why do you think Adam and Eve listened to the snake?

Everything goes wrong

Adam and Eve had children. And their children had children. Soon there were lots of people in the world.

But the people did not trust God. They did very bad things. Everything was going wrong.

God's good world was broken.

The Lord saw that men and women on the earth had become very bad... The Lord was sorry that he had made humans and put them on the earth. He became very upset.

(Genesis chapter 6 verses 5-6, EASY)

blue writing

Noah and the flood

(Genesis chapter 6 verse 9 - chapter 9 verse 17)

God saw all the bad things people were doing. He wanted to get rid of all the bad things and start again.

There was one man who still trusted God and tried to live his way. The man's name was Noah.

God decided to send a flood to cover the earth. He would save Noah's family and start again with them.

God told Noah to build a big boat. *called an Ark* He told Noah to put animals and birds onto the boat. *Ark* Noah did everything God told him to do.

When the flood came, all the other people and animals died. But the people and animals on the boat were safe. *Ark*

After the flood, God made a promise. He said, "I will never again destroy every living thing on the earth as I did this time." (Genesis chapter 8 verse 21, ERV)

Why not use the word Ark? The story of Noah's Ark is still quite well known in kids books

 God wants me to trust him like Noah did. God made me and he loves me. He knows the best way for me to live.

Ask God to help you trust him. Ask him to help you live his way.

After the flood

Noah kept trying to live God's way. But even Noah did bad things sometimes. In the end, most of Noah's family turned away from God, just like everyone else.

The flood had not fixed the world. There was still good in the world, but there was bad in the world too. This was not how God wanted it to be.

What are some bad things in the world?

How do you think God feels about these things?

God wants good things for me. He made me. So he knows the best way for me to live.

I do bad things sometimes, like Adam and Eve. But if I say sorry, God always forgives me. He never stops loving me.

Is there anything you need to say sorry to God for today? Talk to him about it now.

The big story...

Everything had gone wrong. People had turned away from God.

But God still loved people. He had a plan to fix the world.

One day, Jesus would come to help us. He would make a way for people to come back to God.

 Quick look

God has an enemy called the devil.

He wants to pull people away from God.

People trusted the devil instead of God. They did what God said not to do. This is called sin.

The world is broken because of sin.

God had a plan to fix the world.

One day, Jesus would beat the devil.

God's enemy

God is good and strong. He is in charge of everything. But God has an enemy called the devil.

The devil hates God. He hates everything good. The devil wants people to hate God too. He wants to pull people away from God.

The snake who lied to Adam and Eve was the devil. (Page xxx) He told them God was not good. He told them to do what God said not to do.

Adam and Eve believed the devil instead of God.

Adam and Eve were made to be God's friends. They were made to live his way. But they turned away from God. They did what God said not to do.

Sin and death

→ Goodness comes from God.

God made the world good. But now people had done something bad. This let sin into the world.

Sin is the bad things we do. And it is the thing inside us that makes us do bad things. Sin comes from the devil.

This makes it sound like the devil is in us

→ Life comes from God.

God made people and gave them life. But now people had turned away from God. This let death into the world.

Without God, people cannot live forever. This is why people die. Death comes from the devil.

 God → goodness and life

 The devil → sin and death

The world is broken

Because of sin, the world stopped working the way God wanted. Things are not the way they should be. The world is broken.

Sin hurts people too. It is inside all of us. Sin stops us from living God's way.

The Bible says there is a fight going on inside each person. We cannot stop doing bad things, even if we try.

Sin rules me as if I were its slave. I don't understand why I act the way I do. I don't do the good I want to do, and I do the evil I hate.

(Romans chapter 7 verses 14-15, ERV)

blue?

God's plan to fix the world

Sin is a big problem. People cannot fix it. But from the start, God had a plan.

When God sent Adam and Eve out of the garden, he said something to the snake, who was the devil.

God said, "I will make you and the woman enemies to each other. You will bite her child's foot, but he will crush your head." (Genesis chapter 3 verse 15, ERV)

God meant that one day, a person from Adam and Eve's family would fight the devil and beat him. God was talking about Jesus.

The devil would hurt Jesus. But Jesus would beat the devil. This would fix the problem of sin. Then God would fix the world.

The world was broken. But God promised it would not be broken forever. The end of the story would be good.

God chose Abraham and Sarah to start a new family. This family would help God fix the world.

 Genesis chapters 12-50

 **Abraham** (Abram)
Sarah (Sarai)
Isaac
Jacob (Israel)
Joseph

God promised Abraham that he would have a big family.

His family would help God do good things for the world.

Abraham and Sarah were old. But God made something amazing happen.

They had a son called Isaac!

HELLO
my name is

Israel

Isaac had a son called Jacob. God gave Jacob the name Israel.

Jacob's family were called the Israelites. They were God's special people.

Promises from God

God had a plan to fix the world. He wanted some people to help him with his plan.

So God looked at all the people from Noah's family. God chose a man called Abram and his wife Sarai.

Abram and Sarai were old. They did not have any children. But God chose them to be the start of a new family. God wanted this family to show his love to the world.

God told Abram to trust him. He took Abram outside to see the stars. Then God made 3 promises to Abram.

→ A big family.

God promised that Abram would have a big family. There would be as many people in his family as there were stars in the sky!

→ A new home.

God promised to give Abram's family a land to live in.

→ Good things for the world.

God promised that Abram's family would help him do good things for the whole world.

Abram trusted God. He believed that God would keep his promises.

God led Abram outside and said, "Look at the sky. See the many stars. There are so many you cannot count them. Your family will be like that." Abram believed the Lord, and because of this faith the Lord accepted him as one who has done what is right.

(Genesis chapter 15 verses 5-6, ERV)

blue?

 Do you think it was easy or hard for Abraham to believe God's promise?

An impossible baby

God changed Abram's name to Abraham. This name means 'Father of many children'. God also changed Sarai's name to Sarah.

Then God said Abraham and Sarah would would have a baby!

This made Sarah laugh. It was impossible! She and Abraham were too old to have a baby.

But God made it happen! Abraham and Sarah had a son. Now Sarah laughed because she was so happy.

Abraham and Sarah called their son Isaac. This name means 'Someone who laughs'.

What did Sarah's name mean?

The Israelites

When Isaac grew up, he had a son called Jacob.

One night, Jacob was asleep. Then a man came and fought with him. Jacob fought back. He held onto the man and did not let go.

The man said to Jacob, "Your name will now be Israel. I give you this name because you have fought with God and with men, and you have won." (Genesis chapter 32 verse 28) Then Jacob knew that the man was God!

God had given new names to Abraham and Sarah. Now God had given Jacob the name Israel. This name means 'Someone who fights with God'.

Jacob had 12 sons. They had children, and their children had children. Soon they were a big family. They were called the people of Israel, or Israelites.

The Israelites were God's special people. God had chosen them to help him fix the world.

Joseph in Egypt

(Genesis chapters 37-50)

Jacob's favourite son was Joseph.

God gave Joseph strange dreams. In the dreams Joseph's family bowed down to him. This made his brothers angry. They sold him to be a slave in a place called Egypt.

Joseph's life in Egypt was very hard. Then one day the king of Egypt had a dream. God showed Joseph what the dream meant.

The dream meant a bad time was coming. Then Egypt would run out of food. So the king put Joseph in charge of saving food. When the bad time came, Joseph had saved lots of food.

There was no food where Joseph's brothers lived. So they came to buy food from Joseph. They bowed down to him. When they found out he was the brother they had sold, they were afraid.

But Joseph was not angry. He knew God had always been with him. And now he was helping lots of people with God's help. Joseph said to his brothers, "You planned to do something bad to me. But really, God was planning good things." (Genesis chapter 50 verse 20, ERV)

Joseph's brothers were sorry for the bad things they had done. So Joseph forgave his brothers. And he brought his whole family to live with him in Egypt.

What does Joseph's story tell you about God?

space to write answers?

It is hard to forgive people when they hurt me. But God wants me to forgive people like Joseph did.

Is there anyone who has hurt you? Ask God to help you forgive them.

Remember, forgiving someone means giving your angry feelings to God. You can forgive someone without being friends with them.

God chooses me, like he chose Abraham. God wants to work with me to make the world better.

That means I can be part of God's plan. I can help him do good things for the world! That is wonderful.

Ask God to show you one good thing you can do today.

The big story...

God promised that Abraham's family would help him do good things for the world.

A long time after this, Jesus would be born into Abraham's family. And Jesus would fix the problem of sin. He would make a way for people to come back to God.

Abraham's family would lead to Jesus. And Jesus would do wonderful things for the world!

Many years later

The Israelites ~~were~~ *became* slaves in Egypt. God saved them. Then he showed them how to live his way.

Exodus
Leviticus
Numbers
Deuteronomy

Moses
Aaron
Miriam

The Israelites were slaves in Egypt.

God saved the Israelites.

He told Moses to lead them out of Egypt. Moses did what God said.

The Israelites lived in the desert.

They learned to trust God. They agreed to live God's way.

Slaves in Egypt

At first, the Israelites had a good time in Egypt. They grew into a very big family.

But this made the other people in Egypt worried. They thought the Israelites might try to take over.

So the king of Egypt made the Israelites work as slaves. And they made a new law. The law said that all the Israelite baby boys must be killed.

It was a very hard and sad time for the Israelites. They cried out to God for help. And God heard them.

The Lord said, "I have seen the troubles my people have suffered in Egypt, and I have heard their cries when the Egyptians hurt them. I know about their pain."

(Exodus chapter 3 verse 7, ERV)

blue?

A baby in a basket

One day, an Israelite woman had a baby boy. She was afraid that the baby would be killed. So she hid him in a basket in the river.

The princess of Egypt found the baby. She named him Moses. She decided to keep him as her own son.

So Moses grew up as a prince. But when he grew up, he saw what was happening to the other Israelites.

Moses was very angry that his people were slaves. But he did not know how to help them.

Moses ran away from Egypt, and looked after sheep in -a place called- Midian.

(this joins p 40 - p 41)

God makes Moses a leader

(Exodus chapters 3-4)

One day Moses saw something strange. There was a bush on fire. But it did not get burnt up! Moses went closer.

Then God spoke to Moses from the bush. He told Moses to lead the people of Israel out of Egypt!

Moses was afraid. He did not think he could lead the people. He said to God, **"I am not a good speaker… I speak slowly and don't use the best words."** (Exodus chapter 4 verse 10, ERV)

Moses wanted God to send someone else! But God had chosen Moses. He knew Moses was the right person for this job.

So God promised to help Moses. God told Moses's brother Aaron to help him too. Moses said yes. With God's help, Moses became a great leader!

When I have to do something hard, I feel afraid, like Moses. I feel like I cannot do it.

But God always wants to help me. With God's help, I can do everything he wants me to do.

Do you have to do something hard this week? Ask God to help you.

God's people are set free!

God gave Moses a message for the king of Egypt. Moses asked the king to let the Israelites go away for 3 days to worship God.

But the king said no. He thought he was stronger than God. He made the Israelites work even harder!

Can you use the title Pharoah? – it will be familiar to from "Joseph" musical

So God made terrible things happen to Egypt. God did this to show the king how strong he was. And he did it to save his people.

 The king was very afraid. He told the Israelites to go away and never come back!

God's people were free!

> How do you think the Israelites felt when they were set free?

God's agreement with his people

Moses led the Israelites out of Egypt. His brother Aaron and his sister Miriam helped him.

The Israelites lived in the desert. It was very hot and dry. They were hungry and thirsty. And they did not know where they were going.

The Israelites started to complain. But God showed them they could trust him. He looked after them in the desert. God made food fall from the sky. He made water come out of a rock!

God wanted the Israelites to be his special people. He wanted to give them a new land to live in. He wanted them to help him do good things for the whole world. These were the promises God had made to Abraham.

But God gave the Israelites a choice. They could say yes to God and live his way. Or they could say no and live their own way.

The Israelites said yes to God. (Exodus chapter 19 verse 8) So God gave the Israelites some laws to help them live his way.

 What are some things that God wants people to do?

Is it good when people live this way?

Sometimes I feel like I do not know where I am going. I worry about what might happen in the future.

But I know I can trust God. He looks after me, like he looked after the Israelites. He will show me the right way to go.

Thank God for looking after you. Ask him to show you the right way to go.

Viewpoint changes

1st person

3rd person

The big story...

God wanted the Israelites to show the world how to live his way.

They would not always get this right. They would not always live God's way.

But one day Jesus would be born as an Israelite. Jesus would always live God's way. He would do everything God wanted. And he would fix the problem of sin for good.

 Quick look

God gave the Israelites some laws.

The laws helped the Israelites live God's way.

The Israelites worshipped God in a special place.

They had priests to help them worship God.

The Israelites gave offerings to God.

They gave sin offerings to say sorry for their sin.

One day, Jesus would die to fix the problem of sin for good.

God's laws for the Israelites

God gave Moses some laws for the Israelites. There were laws about how to love God and how to love other people.

→ Love God.

God's laws said the Israelites must only worship him. They must love God more than anything else. And they must keep trying to live his way. They must not worship other gods that were not real.

→ Love other people.

God's laws said the Israelites must be kind to each other. They must help poor people. They must be honest and treat each other fairly. This would make life better for everyone.

God wanted the Israelites to be his special people. He wanted them to be different from all the other people in the world.

God wanted the Israelites to show everyone that God's way was the best way to live.

> [Moses said] "If you listen to these laws, and if you are careful to obey them, the Lord your God will keep his agreement of love with you. He promised this to your ancestors."
>
> (Deuteronomy chapter 7 verse 12, ERV)

blue?

The Tabernacle and the Temple

God wanted to live with the Israelites. He told Moses to build a tent, called the Tabernacle.

The Israelites came to the Tabernacle to worship God. When they moved to a new place, they took it with them.

Later, God gave the Israelites their own land. They built a beautiful building in a city called Jerusalem. This building was called the Temple.

The Temple was made of gold and coloured stones. It was a special new place to worship God.

The Tabernacle and the Temple were looked after by priests. The priests led the Israelites in worshipping God.

God is not just in one place. He is everywhere. But the Tabernacle and the Temple were God's special home, where he lived with his people.

Offerings to God

God's laws said the Israelites must give him offerings. The offerings were gifts to show they loved God and trusted him. It was part of how they worshipped God.

The Israelites did not have money. They grew plants to eat. And they kept animals to eat too.

So God told the Israelites to give him some of these things as offerings. Most offerings were bread, oil or animals.

olive

^ (olive oil rather than oil for machines/cars)

People gave their offerings to a priest. The priest took it into the Tabernacle or the Temple.

First the priest burned part of the offering on a special table to give it to God. The rest of the offering was for all the priests to eat.

This was how the Israelites looked after the priests and paid them for their work.

Today, Christians give money to their churches. Some of that money is to look after the church leaders and pay them for their work.

A way to say sorry

There were lots of different offerings. Some were to thank God. Some were to show they loved him. And some were to say sorry.

The Israelites tried to live God's way. But sometimes they broke his laws. So they had to give offerings to God to say sorry.

This sort of offering was a sin offering. It had to be an animal, unless the person was very poor.

The sin offering reminded the Israelites that sin leads to death. And it reminded them how much God loved them.

→ Sin leads to death.

Goodness and life come from God. So turning away from God leads to death.

In the sin offering an animal had to die. The animal died instead of the person.

So the sin offering reminded the Israelites that sin leads to death.

→ God loves us very much.

God wants to be friends with people. When we turn away from God, he wants to help us come back to him.

The sin offering was a way for God's people to keep coming back to him. God forgave their sin so they could keep being friends with him.

So the sin offering reminded the Israelites how much God loved them.

A better plan

The Israelites gave sin offerings every year. This showed they were sorry for their sin. It showed they loved God and wanted to keep living his way.

But the sin offerings were not meant to go on forever. They were a picture of what would happen in the future. God had a better plan.

One day Jesus would die to take away all the bad things everyone had done. He would be like a sin offering for the whole world.

Then, people who trusted Jesus would be forgiven forever. There would be no more sin offerings. The problem of sin would be fixed for good!

God gave the Israelites a land to live in. But they forgot about God. They stopped living his way.

Joshua
Judges
Ruth
1 Samuel chapters 1-8

Joshua
Ruth
Naomi
Boaz
Samuel

 **Quick look**

After Moses died, Joshua became the leader.

Joshua led the Israelites into their new land.

God said if the Israelites lived his way, things would go well.

But if they did not live his way, things would go wrong.

The Israelites stopped living God's way. Things went wrong. So they asked God for help.

God sent judges to save the Israelites.

The Israelites did not want any more judges. They wanted a strong king.

God said yes.

Joshua becomes the leader

Moses was very old. He knew he was going to die soon. So the people of Israel needed a new leader.

God chose a man called Joshua to be the new leader. Then Moses died.

The Israelites had lived in the desert for 40 years. But now it was time for God to give them a new land to live in.

There was a land nearby called Canaan. The people who lived there were doing very bad things.

So God decided punish the people of Canaan. God decided to give their land to the Israelites.

God told Joshua to lead the Israelites into the new land. The Israelites fought the people of Canaan. God helped the Israelites take over the land.

A promise and a warning

The Israelites were made up of 12 big families. They were the families of Israel's 12 sons.

God gave each family a place to live in the land of Israel.

God told his people not to do the bad things the Canaanites had done.

The Israelites had agreed to keep God's laws and live his way. So God gave them a promise and a warning. (Deuteronomy chapter 28)

→ God's promise

If the Israelites lived God's way, things would go well for them.

God would look after them and keep them safe. They would have a good life in their land.

→ God's warning

If the Israelites did not live God's way, things would go wrong for them.

God would not look after them or keep them safe. They would be attacked by their enemies. They would lose their land.

The time of the judges

God's people had a good life in the land of Israel. But they forgot about God. They did not keep God's laws. They did not live God's way. They did whatever they wanted.

So things went wrong for the Israelites. Strong kings from other places attacked them and treated them badly.

When the people were in trouble, they remembered God again. They cried out to God for help.

God never stopped loving his people. Every time the Israelites needed help, God chose a judge to save them.

The most famous judges were Deborah, Samson and Gideon. They tried to lead Israel well.

But the people kept forgetting God. They did not keep God's laws. They did not live his way. They did whatever they wanted.

In those days Israel didn't have a king. The people did anything they thought was right.

(Judges chapter 21 verse 25, NIrV)

Why do you think the Israelites kept forgetting God?

What might have helped them remember God?

Ruth the good friend

(Ruth chapters 1-4)

There were some Israelites who were still living God's way.

A woman called Ruth was looking after her mother-in-law Naomi. Naomi was sad because her husband and sons had died. Naomi and Ruth were very poor.

A rich man called Boaz had a field nearby. He knew that Ruth had come from far away. She had left her own home to be with Naomi.

Ruth was a good friend. And she trusted God. So Boaz helped Ruth and Naomi. He let her pick grain in his fields. He made sure they had enough to eat.

Boaz thought Ruth was very special. So Boaz and Ruth got married. They looked after Naomi together. And they had a baby boy. This made Naomi very happy.

Ruth and Boaz were kind people. God wants me to be kind too. He wants me to look for ways to help other people.

Ask God if there is someone he wants you to help today.

The Israelites ask for a king

The last judge of Israel was Samuel. Samuel trusted God. He tried to live God's way.

But the Israelites did not want to have any more judges. They wanted to have a strong king like everyone else.

This made God sad. His people did not trust him.

God wanted the Israelites to show the world a better way to live. But they just wanted to be like everyone else.

So God gave Samuel a message for the Israelites. Samuel told them that the sort of king they wanted would treat them badly. He said, "When that time comes, you will cry because of the king you chose." (1 Samuel chapter 8 verse 18)

But the Israelites did not listen. They still wanted a king. So God agreed. He said he would give them a king.

> Why do you think the Israelites wanted a strong king?
>
> Why did this make God sad?

Sometimes living God's way makes me different from other people. This is hard. Sometimes I just want to be like everyone else.

But God says it is okay to be different. He wants me to show people that living his way is good.

Ask God to help you live his way, even when it makes you different from other people.

The big story...

God promised to give Abraham's family a land to live in. Now God had kept this promise.

The Israelites were not good at living God's way. But even when they forgot God, God did not forget them. He did not give up on his plan.

Everything that happened was leading to Jesus. And when Jesus came, he would fix the problem of sin for good.

The first kings of Israel

The first 3 kings of Israel were Saul, David and Solomon. After this, God's people split into 2 kingdoms.

1 Samuel chapters 9-31
2 Samuel
1 Kings chapters 1-12
1 Chronicles
2 Chronicles chapters 1-9

Saul
Samuel
David
Solomon

Quick look

The first king of Israel was Saul.

Saul was the sort of king the people wanted. But he turned away from God.

God chose David to be the next king of Israel.

David tried to live God's way.

Solomon was the next king.

God made him very wise and rich.

Later, Solomon turned away from God.

Israel split into 2 kingdoms because of Solomon's sin.

not sure if this is correct?

Saul becomes king

God chose a man called Saul to be the first king of Israel.

Saul was tall, strong and good looking. He was the sort of king the Israelites wanted.

Samuel called all the people together. He made Saul their king.

At first, Saul lived God's way. But then he started to turn away from God.

God saw that Saul did not trust him any more. God decided to find a new king.

God chooses David

God sent Samuel to meet a man called Jesse. Jesse came from Boaz and Ruth's family. He lived in Bethlehem.

God told Samuel the new king would be one of Jesse's sons.

Samuel met 7 of Jesse's sons. They were tall, strong and good looking. Samuel thought God must have chosen one of them. But God said no.

Jesse had one more son. The last son's name was David. He was the youngest. He was looking after his family's sheep.

God told Samuel that David would be the next king of Israel. David would become king after Saul died.

> The Lord said to Samuel… "God doesn't look at what people see. People judge by what is on the outside, but the Lord looks at the heart."
>
> (1 Samuel chapter 16 verse 7, ERV)

David and Saul

God had chosen David to be the next king. But for now, Saul was still king.

David wanted to help Saul. He did whatever Saul told him to do.

When Saul was upset, David played music on his harp. This helped Saul feel better.

All the people loved David. But that made Saul jealous and afraid.

Saul thought David wanted to kill him and take over as king. This was not true. But Saul decided to kill David before David could kill him.

So David ran away. He hid from Saul.

 Saul was the sort of king the people wanted. David was the sort of king God wanted. How were these 2 kings different?

David is kind to Saul

(1 Samuel chapter 24)

Saul and his army were looking for David to kill him. They were a long way from home. Saul needed the toilet. So he went into a cave by himself.

David and his followers were hiding in the cave! They saw Saul come in. But Saul did not see them.

David's followers said, "Saul is alone! Now you can do what you want to him!" They thought David would kill Saul. But David only cut a piece off Saul's clothes.

Later, Saul was with his army. David came out of the cave and called to Saul.

David showed Saul the piece he had cut off Saul's clothes. David said, "I could have killed you. But I did not do it!"

Then Saul was sorry. He said, "You were good to me, even though I have been bad to you." (1 Samuel chapter 24 verse 17, ERV)

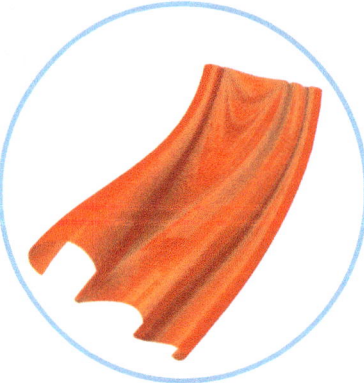

David was kind to Saul because he trusted God. He knew that God would look after him.

God wants me to trust him like David did. He wants me to always be kind, even when it is hard.

When is it hard for you to be kind? Talk to God about this. Ask him to help you.

Remember, being kind does not mean letting people treat you badly. If someone is treating you badly, tell a person you trust.

King ~~David and~~ King Solomon 67

When Saul died, David became king.

David was king for a long time. He trusted God and tried to live God's way. Israel was safe and peaceful while David was king.

When David died, his son Solomon became king.

God spoke to Solomon in a dream. He told Solomon to ask for anything he wanted.

Solomon knew he had an important job. He wanted to be a good king. So he asked God for wisdom. This would help him to make good choices and lead Israel well.

God was very pleased with Solomon. God made Solomon very wise and very rich. Solomon became famous. Everyone came to him for advice.

 Why do you think God was pleased with Solomon?

Solomon turns away from God

Later, Solomon married lots of women. This was something God had said kings must not do. (Deuteronomy chapter 17 verse 17)

Some of Solomon's wives were not Israelites. They worshipped other gods that were not real. So Solomon started worshipping other gods too.

This was a very bad sin. God was very angry. He said Solomon's son would not be king of Israel. *this doesn't make sense*

When Solomon died, his son Rehoboam became king. But Rehoboam was not kind to the Israelites. *wanted to become king of all Israel, but .....*

10 of the families of Israel did not want Rehoboam to be their king. Those families chose a new king, called Jeroboam.

But the other 2 families of Israel kept Rehoboam as their king.

So God's people split into 2 kingdoms, with 2 kings. This happened because of Solomon's sin.

68
67

Sometimes I feel like I am not good enough. I wish I was strong or clever or good looking.

But God does not care about these things. God looks at my heart. He sees what sort of person I am. - inside.
?

God sees that I want to live his way and show his love to people. That is the most important thing.

What do you think God sees when he looks at your heart? Ask God to make you the sort of person who wants to live his way, like David.

The big story...

God promised David that someone from his family would be king forever. (2 Samuel chapter 7 verses 12-13)

God was talking about Jesus. One day, Jesus would be born into David's family.

David was a good king. But even he did bad things sometimes.

But Jesus would be a perfect king. And he would be king forever.

 **Quick look**

There are different sorts of writing in the Bible. We read them in different ways.

Stories normally tell us about things that happened. We can read them like a newspaper.

Reading poems, songs and sayings is like listening to other people who trusted God.

Prophecies are like a picture that shows us how God sees things.

Letters were sent to Christians. They teach us more about Jesus.

66 books

The Bible is made up of 66 books. They were written by different people, at different times and in different places.

There are different sorts of writing in the Bible too. There are lots of stories. But there are also songs, letters and prophecies.

When we read the Bible, it helps to know what sort of writing we are reading. Then we can understand it better.

Understanding the Bible helps us get to know God better. It helps us live his way.

> Everything that is written in the Bible comes from God's Spirit. It helps us in many ways. The Bible teaches us what is true. It warns us when we are doing wrong things. It shows us what is right. It teaches us how to live good lives.
>
> (2 Timothy chapter 3 verse 16, EASY)

Stories

There are lots of stories in the Bible. Most of them tell us about things that happened. We can read these stories like a newspaper.

There are some made up stories in the Bible too. Jesus told stories to teach people about God.

These stories did not really happen. But they teach us important things about God. They help us understand God better.

Poems, songs and sayings

There are poems, songs and sayings in the Bible. These are not like stories. They are like art or music.

Reading this sort of writing is not like reading a newspaper. It is like hearing from other people who trusted God.

The poems and songs show us how these people felt and what they said to God.

The sayings tell us what they learned from trying to live God's way.

These poems, songs and sayings are helpful for us. They help us think about our own friendship with God. They help us to tell God how we feel and to make good choices in our lives.

Prophecies

In the Bible, God gave messages to people called prophets. These messages were called prophecies. They were about things that were happening at the time and things that would happen in the future.

The prophets gave God's messages to the Israelites.

God spoke to the prophets in strange ways. Today, we are not used to reading prophecies. So they can be confusing to read.

Prophecies are not like a newspaper. They are more like a big, colourful picture or a play on a stage.

They help us see things the way God sees them.

Letters

21 of the books in the Bible are letters. They were written to Christians and churches in different places.

Some of the letters start with a hello. At the end there are sometimes messages for one or two people in the church.

The letters teach about following Jesus. Sometimes they answer questions from the church too.

Reading a letter is like reading one side of a chat. We might not know what was happening in the church. And we cannot see the questions they asked. That makes it hard to understand some things.

The letters tell us why Jesus died and how we should live as Christians. They are very helpful for us today.

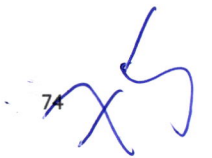

God talks to us

The people who wrote the Bible did not know we would read it so many years later. The world is very different today. But God still uses these 66 books to talk to us.

The Bible says, 'God's word is alive and working. It is sharper than the sharpest sword and cuts all the way into us... It judges the thoughts and feelings in our hearts.' (Hebrews chapter 4 verse 12, ERV)

Sometimes when we read the Bible, one verse might feel more important than the rest. It might feel like a special message for us.

When that happens, we can talk to God about it. We can ask him to help us understand what he is saying to us.

This is one way that God uses the Bible to talk to us.

God's people wrote wisdom books. They help us make good choices and stay close to God.

Job
Psalms
Proverbs
Ecclesiastes
Song of Songs

Job
Solomon
David

Wisdom is being able to make good choices.

There are 5 wisdom books in the Bible.

The wisdom books are like tools for different jobs. They help us at different times.

Job is a story-poem about why bad things happen.

Psalms is a book of songs people sang to God.

Proverbs has wise advice for everyday life.

Ecclesiastes is about the meaning of life.

Song of Songs is about love.

What is wisdom?

Wisdom is being able to make good choices in life.

Life can be confusing. The same choice might be right one time but wrong another time. That is why we need wisdom.

Wisdom helps us think about what we know and work out the best thing to do.

The best way to become wise is to stay close to God. He teaches us how to live his way.

> Trust the Lord completely, and don't depend on your own knowledge. With every step you take, think about what he wants, and he will help you go the right way.
>
> (Proverbs chapter 3 verses 5-6, ERV)

There are 5 wisdom books in the Bible. Some of these books were written in the time of David and Solomon.

The wisdom books are made up of stories, poems, songs and sayings. They ask big questions. They give advice for everyday life. They give us prayers to pray.

These books help us stay close to God and learn how to live his way.

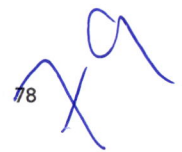

Tools for life

The words of wisdom in these books help us in different ways and at different times.

They are like a bit like tools that we use for different jobs.

In these books we can find wise advice to help us in our own lives.

 What is some wise advice you have learned in your life?

When did this wise advice help you?

Solomon's wisdom

(1 Kings chapter 3 verses 16-28)

King Solomon was very wise. He helped people with very hard problems. He could always work out what to do.

One day 2 women came to see Solomon. They had both had babies. But one of the babies had died. The first woman said the baby who was still alive was hers. But the second woman said that he was hers!

Nobody knew which woman was telling the truth. But Solomon had an idea. He knew how to find out the truth.

 Solomon said he would cut the baby in half. Then the women could have half each!

The first woman said, "All right. Cut him in half." King Solomon saw that the first woman did not care about the baby.

Then the second woman said, "Please, sir, don't kill the baby! Give him to her." (1 Kings chapter 3 verse 26) Even if she could not have the baby, she did not want him to die.

King Solomon saw that that the second woman really loved the baby. He knew she was the baby's mother.

Solomon said, "Give the baby to the woman who loves him."

Everyone was amazed at Solomon's wisdom.

Sometimes life is confusing. I do not know what to do. I need God's help to make a good choice.

God gave Solomon wisdom when he asked for it. God wants to give me wisdom too.

Do you need God's help to make a good choice today? Ask him to give you wisdom.

The wisdom books

Job

 This book is a story-poem about a man called Job.

Everything goes wrong for Job. He is sad and confused. His friends think he is being punished. But God says they are wrong.

This story-poem asks the big question "Why does God let bad things happen?"

It helps us think about the hard times in our lives. It helps us trust God when things go wrong.

Psalms

 This is a big book of songs that the Israelites sang to God. Lots of the songs were written by David.

The songs helped the Israelites tell God if they were feeling happy, sad or angry.

Some of the songs ask questions like "Why are you far away, God?"

This does not mean God is really far away. It is just how the writer felt. It shows we can tell God how we feel too.

Proverbs

This book has wise sayings about everyday life. Solomon wrote lots of the sayings.

The sayings help us think about how to make good choices in different parts of life. They say good things will happen if we make good choices.

This does not mean nothing bad will happen to us. But it means that God's way is the best way to live.

Ecclesiastes

This book is a story-poem. It asks the big question, "What is life all about?" The writer might have been Solomon.

In this story-poem, the writer looks for meaning in life. He decides that lots of the things people care about do not really matter. _ _ _ _ like what?

The writer decides it is good to worship God and enjoy what he gives us. This is the best way to live.

Song of Songs

This book is written as a play. It is about a man and woman who are in love. The writer might have been Solomon.

Most of the play is the man and woman talking to each other. They use word-pictures to talk about how much they love each other.

Song of Songs shows us that love, marriage and sex are good gifts from God.

We can also see the man's love for the woman as a picture of God's love for us.

Can you think of some times when each of these wisdom books might be helpful?

The wisdom books are full of big feelings and big questions. The people who wrote these books knew that God cares about everything in our lives.

I can talk to God about my feelings and questions too. This is part of being friends with him. It helps me get closer to him.

Do you want to tell God how you are feeling? Or do you want to ask him a question? Talk to God about these things now.

The big story...

The wisdom books show us how God's people thought about their friendship with him.

These books were important to Jesus too. When Jesus died on the cross he cried out some words from one of the songs in Psalms. He said, "My God! My God, why have you left me alone?" (Psalms chapter 22 verse 1)

This song was written by David. It has a happy ending when God comes to help.

Jesus knew God would help him too. And he knew his death was part of God's plan to help us all.

The Israelites split into 2 kingdoms. Both kingdoms turned away from God. All God's people lost their land.

1 Kings chapters 13-22
2 Kings
2 Chronicles chapters 10-36

Jereboam
Reheboam
Manasseh
Elijah
Josiah

Now God's people were split into 2 kingdoms.

They were called Israel and Judah.

Israel in the north had bad kings. They turned away from God.

God let Israel's enemies attack them. Israel lost their land.

Judah in the south had good kings and bad kings.

In the end Judah turned away from God too.

God let Judah's enemies attack them. Judah lost their land too.

Some of the people were taken to Babylon.

The 2 kingdoms

Now God's people were split into 2 kingdoms.

Jereboam was king in the north. His kingdom was still called Israel.

Solomon's son Rehoboam was king in the south. His kingdom was called Judah.

Sometimes Israel and Judah helped each other. Sometimes they fought each other.

God's people were supposed to be one big family. They were supposed to show the world how to live God's way. But now they had split apart.

Israel in the north

Jereboam was king of Israel. But God's Temple was in the city of Jerusalem, in Judah. This was there the people worshipped God.

where

This made Jereboam worried. If his people had to go to Judah to worship God, they might want to join Judah again. They might want Reheboam back as their king.

So Jereboam made 2 gold cows. He told his people not to go to the Temple. He told them to worship the cows instead. This was a very bad sin.

All the kings of Israel were like Jereboam. They worshipped gods that were not real. They treated poor people badly. And they led the people away from God. Things got worse and worse in Israel.

God sent prophets to give messages to Israel. He warned them to come back to him before it was too late. But Israel did not listen.

In the end, God let a strong army from Assyria attack Israel. They were beaten. They lost the land God had given them.

> They did not obey God's rules... They did not listen when he warned them... The Lord was so angry with Israel that he sent them far away from himself.
>
> (2 Kings chapter 17 verses 15 and 18, EASY)

Elijah and the fire from heaven

(1 Kings chapter 18 verses 16-45)

God chose Elijah to be his prophet. He told Elijah to warn the king of Israel to live God's way.

The king did not listen. He called Elijah a trouble maker. But Elijah kept doing what God said.

There were some people who worshipped a god called Baal. Elijah wanted to show them that Baal was not real.

So Elijah made a pile of wood and put an offering on it. He told these people to ask Baal to send fire to burn it up. So they prayed to Baal. But fire did not come.

Elijah laughed at them. He said, "Shout louder! Maybe Baal is busy! Maybe he is in the toilet!" They kept trying. But fire still did not come.

Then it was Elijah's turn. He prayed to God. He said, "Please answer me, Lord! Answer me so that these people will know that you, Lord, are the true God." (1 Kings chapter 18 verse 37, EASY)

Then fire came down from the sky! It burned up the wood and the offering! All the people were amazed. They bowed down and said, "The Lord is God!"

God helped Elijah to be brave and stand up for what was right.

God wants me to stand up for what is right too. This can be scary. But I know God will help me.

Ask God to help you be brave and stand up for what is right.

Judah in the south

To start with, things were better in Judah. There were some good kings and some bad kings.

But in the end, things got worse in Judah too. A bad king called Manasseh led the people far away from God. He even came into God's Temple and worshipped other gods there. This was a very bad sin.

God gave his prophets a message for Judah. He said, "Look! I will bring so much trouble against Judah that anyone who hears about it will be shocked." (2 Kings chapter 21 verse 12, ERV)

Later, Judah had a good king called Josiah.

Josiah sent his servants to clean up the Temple. They found a book in the Temple. It was the book of God's laws. It had been lost for a long time. (This book is now the first 5 books of the Bible.)

Josiah was sad when he read the book. He knew the people had broken God's laws. They had stopped living God's way.

Josiah told all the people to come to the Temple. He read the book to them. Josiah promised to live God's way. All the people agreed.

Why did the book of God's laws make Josiah sad?

Why do you think the people broke God's laws?

Babylon attacks

Josiah had done his best. But all the kings after him were bad kings.

These kings led the people away from God again. Things got worse and worse in Judah.

So God let Judah's enemies attack them. The king of Babylon took over Judah. His army burned down Jerusalem and God's Temple. Some of the people were taken away to live in Babylon.

God had warned his people that things would go wrong if they did not live his way. (Page xxx)

Now everything had gone wrong. All God's people had lost their land. And all of this had happened because of their sin.

 Why do you think God let these bad things happen to his people? Was this fair?

Bad kings led Judah away from God. But good kings like Josiah helped them live God's way.

I want to listen to good leaders who love God. I can see that they are living God's way. They can help me live God's way too.

Think about the leaders in your church and where you live. Ask God to help them lead well.

The big story...

Israel and Judah had turned away from God. It looked like God's plan was falling apart.

But God always knew this would happen. He knew people cannot beat sin. We cannot stop doing bad things. We need God's help.

That is why God planned that Jesus would come. Jesus would beat sin for us. He would fix the problem of sin for good.

🔍 **Quick look**

The Bible uses word-pictures to talk about God and the world.

Thinking about a word-picture helps us understand more about God and the world.

The Bible says God looks after us like a shepherd. It says we are like God's sheep.

We see this word-picture lots of times in the Bible. Each time it teaches us something new.

When Jesus talked about himself he used word-pictures that were about God.

Jesus was telling people that he was God!

Pictures in words

The people who wrote the Bible thought about things in pictures. So they used pictures to help readers understand more about God and the world.

But they did not draw these pictures. They wrote about them in words. They said things like 'God is my rock.' (Psalms chapter 18 verse 2, NIrV)

This is a word-picture. God is not really a rock. But thinking about a rock helps us understand something about what God is like.

First, we can picture a rock in our own mind. Then we can ask ourselves 2 questions:

→ What is a rock like?

A rock is big and strong. It does not change or move or break. You can stand on a rock. You can hold onto it or hide behind it.

→ How is God like a rock?

God does not change or move or break. He always stays the same. This means we can trust him. If we hold onto him we will be safe.

Really good explanation

A shepherd and his sheep

Sometimes we see the same word-picture in different parts of the Bible. Each time we see it, we understand more about what it means.

One word-picture says God is a shepherd, and we are his sheep. We see this lots of times in the Bible. Each time, it teaches us something new about our friendship with God.

> The Lord is God. He made us, and we belong to him. We are his people, the sheep he takes care of.
>
> (Psalms chapter 100 verse 3, ERV)

→ God looks after us

David was a shepherd before he was king. He wrote a song about God looking after him like a shepherd. (Psalms chapter 23)

→ When we go our own way we get lost

Later, God said his people were like sheep who did not follow their shepherd. They had gone their own way and got lost. (Isaiah chapter 53 verse 6)

→ God leads us the right way

God also said his people's leaders were bad shepherds. But God would be a good shepherd for his people. (Ezekiel chapter 34)

Jesus is God!

Jesus used the word-picture of a shepherd and his sheep too.

Jesus told a story about a shepherd who looked everywhere for his lost sheep. (Luke chapter 15 verses 3-7)

Jesus said this shepherd was like God. God does not give up on people who turn away from him and get lost.

Later, Jesus said something amazing. He said, "I am the good shepherd, and the good shepherd gives his life for the sheep. (John chapter 10 verse 11, ERV)

Then Jesus said his people would listen to him and follow him like sheep. (John chapter 10 verse 27)

God's people had seen this word-picture before. They knew the Bible said God was their good shepherd. So when Jesus said he was the good shepherd, he was telling them something new.

Jesus was saying that he was God! And he was going to die to save them.

Some more word-pictures

Here are some more word-pictures. Think about these pictures and what they might mean.

'Lord, you are my light.'
(Psalms chapter 27 verse 1, ERV)

→ What is light like?

What does light do? How does it help us?

→ How is God like a light?

'Kind words are like honey.'
(Proverbs chapter 16 verse 24, ERV)

→ What is honey like?

How does honey taste? How is it good for us?

→ What are kind words like?

How does it feel when someone is kind to you?

→ How are kind words like honey?

'Jesus said, "I am the bread that gives life."'
(John chapter 6 verse 35, ERV)

→ What is bread like?

How do we use bread? What does it do for us?

→ How is Jesus like bread?

Before Israel and Judah lost their land, God sent prophets to warn them. The people did not listen. But one day a saviour king would come to to help them.

Isaiah
Jeremiah chapters 1-36
Hosea
Joel
Amos
Obadiah

Jonah
Micah
Nahum
Habakkuk
Zephaniah

Hosea
Isaiah
Jonah
Amos
Jeremiah
Micah
Habakkuk
Nahum
Obadiah

Not very clear that the first list is books of the bible, & second list is names of prophets

Quick look

God sent prophets to warn his people that he would punish their sin.

The people did not listen. But what the prophets said was true.

God said the people had stopped loving God. And they had stopped loving each other.

God sent prophets to warn Israel to treat each other fairly.

God sent prophets to warn Judah to come back to him.

God sent prophets to other places too.

The prophets had some good news too.

One day God would send a saviour king to help his people.

God's prophets

Before Israel and Judah lost their land, God sent prophets to give them messages, called prophecies.

> "Before you were born, I chose you for a special work. I chose you to be a prophet… You must go everywhere I send you and say everything I tell you to say."
>
> (Jeremiah chapter 1 verses 5 and 7, ERV)

The prophets warned the people that God was angry with them. The people had turned away from God. They had broken their promise to him.

The prophets told the people to come back to God and live his way. If they did not live God's way, things would go wrong for them.

Being a prophet was hard. The people did not like what the prophets said! So the prophets did not have many friends. Some of the prophets were killed.

But the things they said were true. In the end, God's people lost their land because of their sin.

What was hard about being a prophet?

What was good about it?

Different sorts of prophecies

Some of the books in the Bible were written by God's prophets. They wrote about what God said to them and what he told them to do.

Some of the prophecies had 2 meanings. One meaning was about what was happening at the time. The other meaning was about what would happen in the future.

God gave his prophets different sorts of prophecies to help the people understand his message.

→ Stories and word-pictures

In one prophecy, God said the people were like a garden where he had planted fruit trees.

God wanted his people to grow good fruit like kindness. But they had grown bad fruit like greed and selfishness. This was because they did not live God's way. (Isaiah chapter 5 verses 1-7)

→ Dreams and visions

God talked to the prophets in dreams and visions. A vision is like a dream you have while you are awake.

In dreams and visions, the prophets saw things the way God sees them. Sometimes God gave them visions of heaven.

→ Actions

Sometimes God told his prophets to do something strange for the people to see. This was a way of acting out the message.

2 important messages

Long ago, God had given his people laws. The laws told God's people how to love him and how to love each other. They had promised to keep these laws. (Page xxx)

Now, God's people had stopped keeping his laws. So he gave his prophets 2 important messages for them.

→ Stop worshipping other gods

God's people had promised to only worship God. But now they worshipped other gods that were not real.

God said they were like a wife who cheated on her husband. He told Hosea to act out this message. Hosea married a woman who cheated on him. This was a picture of what God's people had done.

Hosea said, "Come back to the LORD… The Lord says, 'I will forgive them for leaving me. I will show them my love. " (Hosea chapter 14 verses 1 and 4, ERV)

→ Stop treating each other badly

God's people had promised to be kind to each other and help poor people. But now they treated each other badly.

God told Isaiah the people were like fruit trees he had planted. He wanted them to grow good fruit like kindness. But they had grown bad fruit like greed and selfishness.

God said, "Learn to do good. Treat people fairly… Speak up for the widows and orphans. If you listen to what I say, you will get the good things from this land.." (Isaiah chapter 1 verses 17 and 19, ERV)

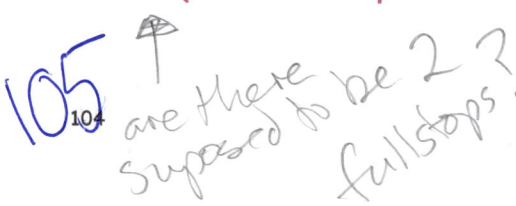

Jonah runs away from God

(Jonah chapters 1-4)

God sent Jonah to take a message to a place called Nineveh. This city was in the land of Assyria. The people there did not know God. They were doing bad things. God was going to punish them.

Jonah did not want to take God's message to the people of Ninevah. He thought they might say sorry. They might stop doing bad things. Then God might forgive them!

Jonah did not want this to happen. He did not like the people of Ninevah! He wanted God to punish them.

So Jonah ran away from God. He got on a boat to go away from Ninevah.

God sent a bad storm. Jonah ended up in the water. Then God sent a big fish to swallow Jonah!

Inside the fish, Jonah said sorry to God. He said he would do what God wanted. God made the fish throw Jonah up onto land.

So Jonah took God's message to Ninevah. The people said sorry. They stopped doing bad things. And God forgave them.

This made Jonah very angry. He complained to God. But God said he loved the people of Nineveh. God wanted to help them, just like he helped the people in Israel and Judah.

God loves everyone. He loves people who do bad things. He even loves people I do not like.

God wants me to try to love people like he does.

Is there anyone you do not like? Ask God to do good things for them. Ask him to help you love them like he does.

Remember, this sort of love means wanting good things for someone. It does not mean you have to be friends with them.

Messages for different places

Messages for Israel

God sent Hosea and Amos to be his prophets in Israel.

Amos said the people gave offerings to God but treated poor people unfairly. God would punish them for this. The offerings did not mean anything if the people were not trying to live God's way.

Messages for Judah

God sent Isaiah and Jeremiah to be his prophets in Judah. He also sent Micah, Joel, Zephaniah and Habakkuk.

After Israel lost their land, Jeremiah warned Judah to come back to God. He said if they kept worshipping other gods, they would lose their land too.

Micah reminded the people what it meant to live God's way. He said people should act fairly and always want to be kind. They should not worry about being important. And they should stay close to God. (Micah chapter 6 verse 8, ERV)

Habakkuk was sad that people were treating each other badly. He asked God how long he would let this go on. God told Habakkuk to trust him. One day he would set things right.

Messages for other places

☒ God gave Jonah, Nahum and Obadiah messages for people in other places.

When Jonah took God's message to Assyria, the people there were sorry. But later they started doing very bad things again. Then their army attacked Israel in the north.

After this, God gave Nahum a new message for Assyria. God said he would punish them for these things.

God also gave Obadiah a message for a place called Edom. The people of Edom were happy when God's people lost their land. God said he would punish them for this.

Good news!

Most of God's prophecies were warnings. But he gave the prophets some good news too.

God said that one day, he would send a saviour king to help his people. He would make a way for them to come back to him.

Isaiah wrote down what God told him about the saviour king. He wrote, "He carried our pain for us.. It was our sins that caused his wounds… The punishment that he received has brought peace to us." (Isaiah chapter 53 verses 4-5)

This meant that the saviour king would die to take away the bad things everyone had done. He would fix the problem of sin for good.

When everything went wrong, this message gave God's people hope. Even though they had turned away from God, God still loved them. He still had a plan to fix the world.

Why do you think this message gave God's people hope?

Do you know who the saviour king is? Can you guess?

God's people did not like all his messages to them. But God gave these messages because he loved his people. He wanted to help them live his way.

I read God's messages in the Bible. I hear them in talks at church and in other ways too.

Some of God's messages are hard to hear. But if I listen, they help me live his way.

Ask God to help you listen to him even when his message is hard.

The big story...

God was starting to show people more of his plan.

A saviour king would come from David's family. He would live God's way and die to take away all the bad things everyone had done.

These prophecies did not tell people the name of the saviour king. But they were talking about Jesus.

From the start, God had planned for Jesus to come and save us. Jesus was the only person who could fix the problem of sin.

10   God punishes his people

Many of the people of Judah were taken to Babylon.
They had lost their land. But God was still with them.

Jeremiah chapters 37-52
Lamentations
Ezekiel
Daniel

again not very clear

The prophets were:—

Ezekiel
Daniel

Israel and Judah had turned away from God. Now they had lost their land.

God had warned them this would happen.

The people of Judah were called Jews. Some of them were taken to Babylon.

The Jews knew this had happened because of their sin. They were very sorry. They wanted to change.

The Jews thought God had left them. But God gave Ezekiel a vision of dry bones coming back to life.

This meant God would make a way for the Jews to come back to him.

God's people lose their land

Long ago, the Israelites had agreed to live God's way. (Page xxx)

Then God had given them a land to live in. And he had given them a promise and a warning. (Page xxx)

God said if the Israelites lived his way, he would keep them safe. But if they did not live his way, he would not keep them safe. They would lose their land.

The Israelites did not live his way. They split into 2 kingdoms. And they turned away from God again and again.

God was patient for a long time. He kept his people safe. And he sent prophets to warn them to come back to him.

But in the end, God did what he said he would do. He stopped keeping his people safe. He let enemies attack them. They lost their land.

Now, the king of Assyria had taken over Israel. Some of the people of Israel were taken to Assyria.

The king of Babylon had taken over Judah. Some of the people of Judah were taken to Babylon. The people of Judah were called the Jews.

Life in Babylon

Living in Babylon was hard for the Jews. They had to do what the king of Babylon said. They were not free. They could not go home.

The Jews had lost God's Temple too. They could not worship God in the way he wanted.

The Jews knew all this had happened because of their sin. They were very sad.

The Jews lived in Babylon for 70 years. They thought about the bad things they had done. They were very sorry. They wanted to change. They wanted to live God's way.

 How did the Jews end up in Babylon?

How did living in Babylon change them?

Daniel and the lions

(Daniel chapter 6)

One of the Jews who was taken to Babylon was called Daniel. Daniel was young and strong. So the king of Babylon gave him an important job.

Daniel was very good at his job. This made the king's other workers jealous. They wanted to get rid of him.

The workers knew Daniel prayed to God 3 times every day. So they said to the king, "We think everyone should only pray to you for 30 days. If they pray to anyone else they should be thrown to the lions!" The king liked this idea. He made it the law.

this sentence might read better the other way round

Daniel heard about the new law. But he loved God. He knew God did not want him to pray to the king. So Daniel kept praying to God. And the other workers saw him. They told the king.

The king was very sad. He liked Daniel. But he followed his law. Daniel was thrown to the lions. He was in the lions' den all night.

In the morning, Daniel was still alive! He said to the king, "It is okay! God kept me safe because he knew I had done nothing wrong."

The king was very happy. He made another new law. He told all the people to worship Daniel's God!

The law told Daniel to do something bad. Sometimes people tell me to do bad things too.

But God wants me to keep doing the right thing, like Daniel. I can trust God to look after me.

Has anyone ever told you to do something bad? Talk to God about this. Ask him to help you do the right thing.

Hope for the Jews

The Jews thought God had left them. But God still loved his people. He had not given up on his plan.

God gave a message to a prophet called Ezekiel. God showed Ezekiel a vision of dry bones.

The bones were from people who had been dead for a long time. But God told Ezekiel to tell the bones to come back to life.

Ezekiel did what God said. The bones became living people again!

This vision had a special meaning for the Jews. They had lost everything. They felt like those dry, dead bones.

But God wanted the Jews to know he was still with them. God said that one day he would bring them home to Judah. He would save them from their sin. And he would make a way for them to come back into his goodness and life.

"I will make you completely pure and 'clean'… I will give you hearts that obey me. I will put my Spirit in you… You will be my people. And I will be your God."

(Ezekiel chapter 36 verses 25-28, NIrV)

Ezekiel's vision gave the Jews hope. What gives you hope when life is hard?

When I do bad things, it hurts me and other people. Even when God forgives me, the hurt does not always go away.

But it is never too late to start again. When I say sorry, God helps me move on and make better choices.

Every day I have a new chance to live God's way. Living God's way is good for me and good for the world!

Thank God for giving you a new start. Ask him to help you live his way today.

The big story…

The Jews really wanted to change. But God knew they could not change themselves. They could not beat sin on their own.

That is why they needed Jesus, the saviour king. But there was more to God's plan!

God told Ezekiel his Holy Spirit would come to live inside people. The Holy Spirit would change their hearts. He would help them live God's way.

11 God's people come home

After 70 years, the Jews were allowed to go home.
Later, Nehemiah started to build Jerusalem again.

Nehemiah
Ezra
Haggai
Zechariah
Esther
Malachi

Haggai
Zechariah
Ezra
Esther
Nehemiah

again not very clear, and they are in a different order and where is Malachi in the 2nd list?

 **Quick look**

repetition

After 70 years, the Jews were allowed to go home. <u>Some</u> went home, but <u>some</u> stayed.

<u>Some</u> Jews went to Jerusalem. They started to build the Temple again.

Haggai and Zechariah told the Jews to come back to God. Ezra led them in worship.

Later, Nehemiah went to build the walls of Jerusalem again.

In the end, lots of Jews went home to Judah.

The Jews promised to live God's way.

Some Jews go home

After 70 years, the king of Persia took over Babylon. He said the Jews could go home!

> King Cyrus… said: 'The Lord, the God of heaven… has said that I must build a temple for him in Jerusalem… Any of God's people who live among you may now return to Jerusalem.'
>
> (2 Chronicles chapter 36 verses 22-23, EASY)

By then, most of the Jews who had been taken to Babylon had died. Their children had lived in Babylon all their lives. Some went to live in the land of Judah. But some stayed.

Jerusalem was still ~~broken down~~ in ruins. This was God's special city where the Temple had been. But there was no Temple any more.

Haggai and Zechariah were prophets. They went to Jerusalem. They told the people that God still loved them. If they came back to God, he would do good things for them.

Later, Ezra the priest went to Jerusalem. He led the Jews in worship. He read the book of God's laws to the people.

Other Jews went to Jerusalem too. They started building the Temple again.

Esther saves God's people

(Esther chapters 3-10)

Later, there was a new king in Babylon.

This king chose a woman called Esther to be his wife. He did not know Esther was a Jew. So Esther became queen.

A man called Haman hated the Jews. He lied to the king. He said the Jews were making trouble. He told the king to have them killed. And the king agreed to Haman's plan.

Queen Esther heard about Haman's plan. She was very sad. She wanted to help her people. She wanted to talk to the king.

But Esther was not allowed to talk to the king unless he called for her. So if she went to see him, he might have her killed!

Esther trusted God. She asked all the Jews to pray for her. Then she went to see the king. He was happy to see her!

Esther asked the king and Haman to come to a party. At the party, she told them she was a Jew. And she told the king that Haman had tricked him.

The king was very angry. He had Haman killed! And the Jews were saved! They thanked God. Every year, they remembered Esther at a festival called Purim. Purim is still a festival today!

Lots of people have done brave things to help other people, like Esther did. Can you think of any? If not, ask someone about this.

Esther was only one person. But God worked with her to save lots of people.

God wants to work with me too. He wants me to help him do good things in the world, like Esther did.

Ask God how he wants to work with you. Ask him to show you some good things you can do this week.

Nehemiah builds the walls

Later, a Jew called Nehemiah lived in Babylon. He worked for the king.

Nehemiah heard that the walls of Jerusalem was still broken down. This made him very sad.

The king asked Nehemiah why he was sad. So Nehemiah told him about Jerusalem. He asked the king to let him go and build the walls of Jerusalem again.

The king said yes. So Nehemiah went to Jerusalem. Some other Jews went with him. They worked together. They started to build the walls again.

In the end, lots of Jews came back to Judah. They still had to do what the king in Babylon said. But they were home!

God had promised Ezekiel that he would bring the Jews home. (Page xxx) Now it had happened. God had given them a new start.

The Jews were very happy. They promised to keep God's laws and live his way.

All the people who went to Jerusalem were good at different things. How did each of them help the Jews?

went "the people who went to Jerusalem" "the Jews?"

God has made lots of promises in the Bible. He says he will always be with me. He says he will always forgive me when I say sorry. He says if I trust him, I will live forever with him after I die.

My life is not always easy, but God has done lots of good things for me. And I know I can trust him to keep all his promises.

Think about some of the promises God has made. Thank God for keeping his promises.

The big story…

The Jews were home. But they were still waiting for God to keep his biggest promises.

400 years later, Jesus the saviour king would come. He would die to take away all the bad things everyone had done. This would change everything.

People could not keep all God's laws. So Jesus would make a better way to be friends with God.

People could not change themselves. So God's Holy Spirit would come and change their hearts.

God was going to give everyone a wonderful new start.

🔍 **Quick look**

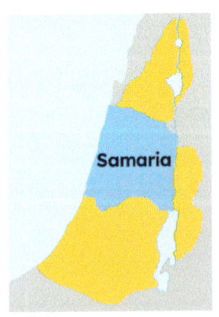

When the Jews came home, people called Samaritans were living in Israel.

Jews did not like Samaritans.

and Samaritans

The Jews were now ruled by the Romans. ^

them.

Life was hard for the ~~Jews~~.

The Jews tried to live God's way.

They were led by 2 groups called the Pharisees and Sadducees.

The Jews were waiting for the saviour king.

They did not know the saviour king would be God himself!

The Bible and history

The Old Testament of the Bible ends with the Jews coming home.

The New Testament starts with Jesus being born.

But there are 2 questions the Bible does not answer.

→ **What happened to the the people of Israel while the Jews were in Babylon?**

Israel in the north was taken over by Assyria. But the Bible does not tell us what happened next.

→ **What happened after the Jews came home?**

There were 400 years between the end of the Old Testament and the start of the New Testament.

These are sometimes called 'the silent years', because the Bible does not talk about them.

History tells us the answers to both these questions. This helps us understand the New Testament better.

Jews and Samaritans

Israel in the north had been taken over by Assyria. (Page xxx) The king of Assyria had moved some people out of Israel. And he had moved people from other places into Israel.

All the people who lived in Israel had mixed together and had children. They lived in a part of Israel called Samaria. They were called Samaritans.

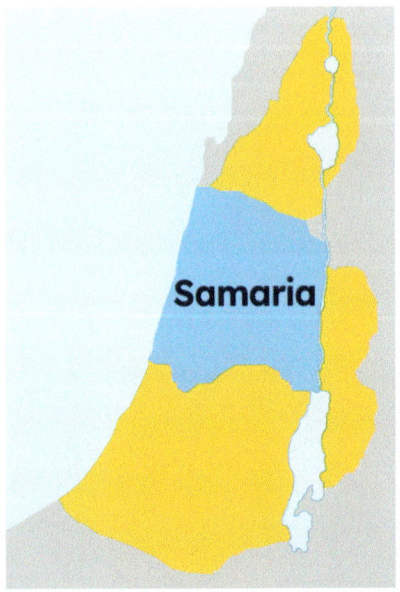

The Jews did not like the Samaritans. They thought the Samaritans were not Israelites because they were mixed with people from other places.

The Samaritans also believed some different things about God. And they worshipped God in a different place.

But when Jesus came, he would be kind to the Samaritans. He would make a way for them to be part of God's people again.

> Jesus said to her, 'You people from Samaria do not know the one that you worship… But people will soon have a new way to worship the Father."
>
> (John chapter 4 verses 22-23, EASY)

Romans take over Israel

The big armies of the world kept fighting each other. While the Jews were in Babylon, Babylon and Assyria were taken over by Persia.

Later, Persia was taken over by Greece. Then Greece was taken over by the Romans. Now the Romans ruled Israel and Judah.

The Jews were back home, but they had to do what the Romans said. The Romans treated the Jews badly. They made the Jews pay lots of money in taxes.

The Romans made a man called Herod king of Judah. King Herod made the new Temple bigger. But he was a bad king. He worked with the Romans.

Life was hard for the Jews. They hated being ruled by the Romans.

130

The Jews try to live God's way

The Jews had done bad things in the past. That was why they had lost their land. But now they were home, they wanted to change. They wanted to live God's way.

The Jews started to meet in buildings called synagogues. Here they prayed and learned about God. They set up schools so children could learn God's laws.

There were teachers who taught people how to live God's way. Sometimes these teachers had students, called disciples.

Disciples followed their teacher and learned from them. Later they might become teachers themselves.

The leaders of the Jews

A group called the Sanhedrin were the leaders of the Jews.

The Sanhedrin was made up of Pharisees, Sadducees and teachers of the law.

→ Pharisees

The Pharisees believed God was close to his people. They said all the books about God were important. (These books are now the Old Testament.)

The Pharisees tried to keep all God's laws. They made lots of extra rules too. They said everyone must follow their rules.

→ Sadducees

The Sadducees believed God was far away. They said only the first 5 books about God were important.

The Sadducees were rich and powerful. Some were priests who led worship at the new Temple. They wanted to keep their power. So they worked with the Romans.

→ Teachers of the law

Teachers of the law helped people make agreements, like getting married or working together. They made sure these agreements followed God's laws.

The people in the Sanhedrin did not always agree. But together they led the Jews. They were still leading the Jews when Jesus came.

God's big surprise

The Jews remembered the promise God had given to the prophets. One day God would send a saviour king to help his people.

The Jews hoped the saviour king would come soon. They hoped he would save them from the Romans.

Soon it would be time for God to keep his promise. But this would happen in a surprising way.

The saviour king was going to be God himself!

God was going to come into the world as a baby. He was going to live with his people as a man called Jesus.

But Jesus was not going to save the Jews from the Romans. He was going to do something much bigger and better. Jesus was going to beat the devil and save everyone from sin.

Jesus would fix the problem of sin. And then God would fix the world!

God was born as a baby called Jesus. When Jesus grew up, he started teaching the Jews about God.

Matthew chapters 1-4
Mark chapters 1-3
Luke chapters 1-5
John chapter 1

Mary
Joseph
Jesus
John the Baptist
Matthew

God came into the world as a baby called Jesus.

Jesus was the saviour king! He was going to fix the problem of sin.

John the Baptist told the Jews to get ready for the saviour king.

He baptised people who wanted to live God's way.

John even baptised Jesus!

Jesus chose 12 men to be his disciples. They went with him everywhere.

Jesus started teaching all the people about God.

Jesus is born

God sent an angel to a woman called Mary. The angel told her she would have a baby boy.

Mary was confused. She had never had sex! But the angel said this baby was from God. He was the saviour king God had promised!

Mary was about to marry a man called Joseph. God sent an angel to him too. The angel told Joseph about the baby. He told Joseph to call the baby Jesus. This name means 'saviour'.

This baby would change everything for Mary and Joseph. But they trusted God. They did what he asked them to do.

> How did Mary and Joseph show they trusted God?
>
> What helps you keep trusting God when things change?

shouldn't the shepherds come first, then the wise men?

When Jesus was born, wise men came to worship him. They had seen a special star that meant a king had been born.

Shepherds came to worship Jesus too. God had sent angels to tell them the saviour king had been born.

When King Herod heard about Jesus, he was worried. He did not want a new king! He wanted to get rid of Jesus. So he told his soldiers to kill all the baby boys in Bethlehem.

God warned Joseph in a dream. He told Joseph to take Mary and Jesus far away. They did not come home until King Herod died.

John the Baptist

Mary's cousin had a special baby too. His name was John. God told his family that John would be a prophet. He would tell people to get ready for the saviour king.

When John grew up, he told everyone that the saviour king was coming soon. He said they must come to God and say sorry for the bad things they had done.

John baptised the people by dipping them in water. This was to show they had promised to live God's way.

Jesus had grown up. He was now a man. And he came to be baptised by John.

John did not want to baptise Jesus. He knew that Jesus had not done any bad things. He was the saviour king! But Jesus said this was what God wanted. So John baptised Jesus.

Then God's Holy Spirit came to rest on Jesus's head. The Holy Spirit looked like a white bird called a dove. The people there heard God say that Jesus was his son.

So Jesus was baptised. As soon as he came up out of the water, the sky opened, and he saw God's Spirit coming down on him like a dove. A voice from heaven said, "This is my Son, the one I love. I am very pleased with him."

(Matthew chapter 3 verses 16-17, ERV)

Jesus's disciples

It was time for Jesus to start his special work. He started to teach people about God. And he healed people who were sick.

Jesus chose 12 men to be his disciples. Most teachers chose disciples who were very clever and knew a lot about God. But Jesus chose normal people.

Some of Jesus's disciples were fishermen. One was a man who wanted to fight the Romans. And one was a man who worked for the Romans!

They were all different. But Jesus chose them all to be his disciples.

Some other men and women followed Jesus too. They went with him wherever he went.

All these people wanted to learn from Jesus. And they helped him tell people about God.

 Why do you think Jesus chose normal people to be his disciples? Is this a surprise?

Jesus chooses a tax man

(Matthew chapter 9 verses 9-13)

Some Jews worked for the Romans. Their job was to get tax money from other Jews. Everyone hated tax men.

Matthew was a tax man. One day he was doing his job. Jesus walked past with his disciples. Then Jesus stopped.

Jesus said to Matthew, "Come and follow me." He wanted Matthew to be one of his disciples! Matthew was very surprised. He left his job and followed Jesus!

Later, Jesus and his disciples had dinner at Matthew's house. There were lots of people there who had done bad things.

The Pharisees were very upset. They thought Jesus should stay away from people who had done bad things.

But Jesus said, "People who are well do not need a doctor. It is people who are ill that need a doctor."

Jesus meant that sin was like an illness. It stopped people living God's way. They could not get better on their own. But Jesus was like a doctor who could help people get better. He could help them live God's way.

Jesus said, "Some people know that they have done wrong things. I am asking those people to come to me for help."
(Matthew chapter 9 verse 13)

well explained

The Pharisees thought they were good people. They did not think they needed help. But the people who had done bad things knew they needed help.

Jesus loves everyone. He even loves people who have done lots of bad things.

Jesus knows we cannot live God's way on our own. He helps everyone who comes to him for help.

needing?

Do you need help to live God's way? Jesus wants to help you too. Ask him to help you now.

Jesus chose his disciples. And he chooses me too.

It does not matter how much I know about God. It does not matter how clever I am. Jesus chooses me as I am.

Jesus wants me to follow him and learn from him. He wants me to try to be like him. And he promises to help me do this.

Tell Jesus how you feel about him choosing you.

The big story...

God had told the prophets some things about the saviour king. These were clues so people would know the saviour king when he came.

God told Isaiah that the mother of the saviour king would be someone who had never had sex. He was talking about Mary!

Then God said the saviour king would be called Immanuel. This means 'God with us'. (Isaiah chapter 7 verse 14) This was a clue that the saviour king would be God himself!

Jesus was God, and he was human too. He was the saviour king God had promised!

Jesus showed the Jews what God is like. They were amazed by what he said and did. But the leaders of the Jews did not like Jesus.

Matthew chapters 5-20
Mark chapters 4-10
Luke chapters 6-18
John chapters 2-11

Jesus
Jairus
Peter

This whole chapter (13)
is excellent.

Lots of people came to listen to Jesus. He told them all about God.

People were amazed by the things Jesus said.

Jesus did amazing things too.

He made lots of sick people better.

Some people believed Jesus was the saviour king.

But the leaders of the Jews did not like Jesus.

The people learn from Jesus

Jesus and his disciples went all around the land of Israel. They even went to Samaria, where the Samaritans lived! Wherever they went, people came to listen to Jesus.

Jesus told stories to help people understand more about God. He told the people what God was like. He told them how good it was to live God's way.

Jesus showed the people how to live God's way. He always did the right thing. He was kind to poor people. He spent time with people who others did not care about.

Jesus was kind to people who had done bad things. He forgave anyone who was sorry. And he told them to start living God's way.

Jesus showed the people how much God loved them. He gave them hope.

Jesus... taught in the synagogues. He preached the good news of God's kingdom. He healed every illness and sickness the people had. News about him spread... Large crowds followed him.

(Matthew chapter 4 verses 23-25, NIrV)

Jesus does amazing things

At that time, it cost lots of money to go to the doctor. And doctors did not know as much as they know now. There were lots of people they could not help.

People who were sick or disabled could not work. So they were very poor. They had to beg for money to buy food.

But Jesus could do amazing things! He made sick people better. He made blind people see. He made disabled people walk.

Jesus did these things to show that God did not just love rich, strong people. He loved poor, sick people too. He loved all people the same.

Jesus did other amazing things too. He stopped a storm. He fed a big crowd with a little bit of bread and fish.

Jesus did all these things to show that he had God's power. Only God could do things like this!

Jesus heals 2 people

(Luke chapter 8 verses 40-56)

An important man called Jairus came to see Jesus. Jairus was the leader of the synagogue, where people went to pray and learn about God.

Jairus was upset. His daughter was very sick. He asked Jesus to come to his house and make her better. So Jesus and his disciples went with Jairus. Lots of people followed them.

On the way, there was a woman who was sick. She had an illness that made her bleed. She had spent all her money on doctors. But she was still sick. She had been sick for 12 years.

The woman knew Jesus could heal her. But she was not important like Jairus. She did not want to get in trouble. So she just touched Jesus's coat. Right away, she stopped bleeding! She was better!

Jesus stopped. He said, "Who touched me?" The woman said it was her. Then Jesus said, "You are well again because you believed in me." (Luke chapter 8 verses 45 and 48, ERV)

Then someone came with a message for Jairus. His daughter had died. But Jesus told Jairus she would be healed.

When they got to the house, Jairus's daughter was dead. Jesus said to her, "Little girl, stand up." (Luke chapter 8 verses 54, ERV) And she got up! Jesus had made her alive again!

The woman with the bleeding illness thought she was not important. But she was important to Jesus.

Jesus loves rich people and poor people. He loves strong people and sick people. He loves them all the same.

Everyone is important to Jesus. So they should be important to me too.

Think about someone who is having a hard time. Ask Jesus how you can show they are important to you.

Peter's Answer

The people loved the amazing things Jesus did. But Jesus did these things to point them to something even more amazing. He was the saviour king they were waiting for!

Not everybody understood this. But some people did.

One day Jesus asked his disciples, "Who do the people think I am?" The disciples said some people thought Jesus was a prophet who had come back to life.

bold?

emphasis needed

Then Jesus asked, "Who do you think I am?"

One of Jesus's disciples was Peter. He knew the answer. Peter said to Jesus, "You are the saviour king!" (Mark chapter 8 verses 27-33)

Jesus was pleased with Peter's answer. Peter understood who Jesus really was.

If you were there when Jesus said and did all these things, what would you think about him?

Jesus upsets the leaders

Lots of the Jews loved Jesus. But their leaders did not trust him.

The Pharisees thought Jesus should stay away from people who had done bad things. They wanted Jesus to follow their rules.

The Pharisees were waiting for the saviour king. But Jesus was not the sort of saviour king they wanted.

The Sadducees were worried about Jesus. They thought Jesus might lead the people to fight the Romans. Then the Sadducees would lose all their power.

Jesus told the leaders that God was not happy with them. He said they were making it too hard for people to follow God. They did not love people like God did.

Jesus told the leaders to change and live God's way. This made them very angry. They did not want the people to listen to Jesus. They wanted to get rid of him.

 Which people liked Jesus and which people did not?

Why do you think this was?

God loved us so much he became a man. So if I want to know what God is like, I can read about Jesus.

Jesus loved everyone. He had power to do amazing things. He forgave people and helped them.

Jesus is God. But he knows what it is like to be human too. He is the best friend I can have.

What does Jesus show you about what God is like? Thank him for these things.

The big story...

The Jews thought the saviour king would beat the Romans and set them free. They did not understand they had another problem that was much bigger.

Sin had broken the world. It kept people away from God's goodness and life.

That was the problem Jesus had come to fix. He was going to beat the devil and set the world free from sin.

Jesus would make a way for everyone to come back to God.

 **Quick look**

Jesus told the people about God's kingdom.

Anyone can be in God's kingdom if they believe Jesus and try to live God's way.

God wants us to love him and love other people.

He wants us to forgive people.

Jesus did things for other people. He wants us to live like this too.

He said money does not make us rich. Doing good things makes us rich in God's kingdom.

Jesus told us to pray for God's kingdom to grow in the world.

Jesus's big message

Jesus had a big message for the people. He said, "God's kingdom is very near. Change your hearts and lives, and believe the Good News!" (Mark chapter 1 verse 15, ERV)

In God's kingdom, God is the king. But God's kingdom is not just one place. It is anywhere people worship God and live his way.

Anyone can be part of God's kingdom. We do not have to be rich, clever or important. There are just 2 things we have to do.

→ Believe Jesus

We must believe that Jesus is the saviour king. And we must believe the things he said.

→ Try to live God's way

We must turn away from sin and come back to God. We must try to live his way. But we must ask God for help to do this. We cannot do it on our own.

Jesus said the way into God's kingdom is trust.

We must trust that God loves us. We must trust that he knows the best way to live. And we must trust him to help us live that way.

A kingdom of love

God's kingdom is built on love. Jesus said everyone in God's kingdom must love God and love people. He said all God's other laws come out of loving God and loving people.

> [Jesus said,] 'You should love the Lord your God with all that you are… This is… the most important of all God's Laws. The second rule is also important… You should love other people as much as you love yourself. All God's Laws that Moses gave us come from these two rules.'
>
> (Matthew chapter 22 verses 37-40, EASY)

Jesus said it is easy to love people who love us. But we must even love people who hate us.

The love Jesus talked about is not a feeling. It is an action. It means thinking about what we want people to do for us, then doing those things for other people. We call this the golden rule. (Matthew chapter 7 verse 12)

Forgiving people

It is easy to see other people's sin. And it is not easy to see our own sin. That can make us think we are better than other people.

Jesus said sin starts in our hearts. So sin is not just the bad things we do. It is also the bad things we think and say.

If we do not do the good things God wants us to do, this is sin too.

We do not all do the same bad things. But we all have sin in our hearts. So we must not think we are better than other people.

God forgives us when we say sorry. But we must also forgive other people when they hurt us. This is part of being sorry. It is part of making God our king. (Matthew chapter 6 verses 13-14)

Forgiving someone does not mean we have to keep being friends with them. It does not mean we have to let them keep hurting us.

Forgiving someone means giving our angry feelings to God. It means not trying to make them pay for what they did.

God wants us to love people who do bad things and people who hurt us. He wants us to pray for them. We can pray that God will help them change.

Living like Jesus

Jesus said we must not show off to other people. We must not do good things to make other people think we are good. We must not try to be important.

Instead, we must only care what God thinks. We must do good things quietly. We must see other people as important.

This is how Jesus lived. He was God, but he became human. He made himself less important. He did not tell people to do things for him. He did things for people.

Once, Jesus washed his disciples' feet. This was a servant's job!

Jesus did this to show his disciples that he wanted them to live like servants. He wanted them to do things for other people, like he did.

Jesus said God's kingdom is not like this world. He said, "One day, those people who are not important now will become the most important." (Matthew chapter 20 verse 16, EASY)

Jesus said if we make ourselves less important, God will make us more important. If we do good things for other people, God will do good things for us.

A warning about money

Jesus said we should not worry about what might happen in the future. Bad things do happen. But we can trust God because he loves us. He will always be with us.

Jesus said we should stay close to God and do what he wants. Then God will give us good things.

Jesus gave a warning about money. Money is not bad. But loving money more than God is very bad.

Some people try to get more and more money. They think money will make them safe. They trust money more than God. They love money more than God. They make money their king.

These people worry about losing their money. They do not give money to people who need it. They keep it all for themselves.

Jesus said people can only have one king. If God is our king, we cannot make money our king as well. (Matthew chapter 26 verses 24-26)

Jesus said we must love and trust God, not money. Then we will not keep all our money for ourselves. We will use it to do what God wants. And we will give money to people who need it.

Jesus said we should not want to be rich in this world. Instead, we should do good things. This makes us rich in God's kingdom.

How to pray

Jesus told his disciples how to pray. He said we should ask Father God for everything we need. And we should keep asking and not give up.

Jesus said Father God listens to our prayers. He knows what will be good for us. And he gives us those good things.

Jesus gave his disciples a prayer to pray. (Matthew chapter 6 verses 9-13) We call this 'The Lord's Prayer'. Some churches pray this prayer every Sunday.

The Lord's prayer reminds us that God is king. It asks God to give us what we need. It asks God to forgive us and keep us safe.

Here is part of the Lord's prayer:

Your kingdom come, your will be done,
on earth, as it is in heaven.

These words ask God to grow his kingdom in the world. They ask God to do what he wants in the world and in our lives.

One day the whole world will be God's kingdom. Then this prayer will be answered forever.

The leaders of the Jews arrested Jesus and killed him! But this was all part of God's plan to fix the world.

Matthew chapters 21-27
Mark chapters 11-15
Luke chapters 19-23
John chapters 12-19

Jesus
Peter
Judas

Quick look

Jesus came to Jerusalem for the Passover festival.

The leaders of the Jews looked for a reason to kill Jesus.

Jesus had a special meal with his disciples. He said the bread and wine were a picture of his body and blood.

Jesus knew he was going to die.

Jesus went away to pray.

Then the leaders arrested him. They told the Romans to kill him.

The Romans nailed Jesus to a wooden cross. Jesus died.

Jesus's disciples *and friends* thought everything had gone wrong.

Jesus in Jerusalem

There was a special festival called Passover. At Passover the people remembered how God had saved them from Egypt long ago. (Page xx)

At Passover everyone went to Jerusalem. They worshipped God and ate together.

Jesus and his disciples went to Jerusalem. It was time for Jesus to show everyone that he was the saviour king.

God had told one of the prophets that the saviour king would ride into Jerusalem on a donkey. (Zechariah chapter 9 verse 9) So that is what Jesus did.

Jesus told the people about God. The leaders of the Jews got more and more angry with him. They looked for a reason to kill him.

Jesus knew what was going to happen. He told his disciples that he would die and then come back to life. But they did not understand.

A special meal

Jesus ate the special Passover meal with his disciples. He gave them bread and wine. He said this was a picture of his body and blood.

Jesus said this because he was going to die soon. This was part of God's plan to save people from sin and fix the world.

We have communion at church to remember that Jesus did this.

After the meal, one of Jesus's disciples left. His name was Judas. The chief priests had given him money to lead them to Jesus.

Jesus is arrested

Later, Jesus went away to pray. Jesus was very upset. He did not want to die. But he knew it was the only way to fix the problem of sin. This was why he had come.

[Jesus] prayed, "Father, if it is possible, please save me from this time of great pain. But Father, I do not ask you to do what I want. Do what you want to do.'

(Matthew chapter 26 verse 39, EASY)

Then Judas came with the servants of the chief priests. They arrested Jesus.

The chief priests and other leaders were angry because Jesus said he was the saviour king. The leaders said this was a lie and a very bad sin. They said Jesus must be killed.

The chief priests took Jesus to the Roman in charge of Jerusalem. His name was Pilate. They said Jesus was making trouble by saying he was a king. They told Pilate to have him killed. And Pilate agreed.

 Some people believed Jesus was the saviour king. Some people did not believe this. What do you think and why?

Peter lies about knowing Jesus

(Matthew chapter 26 verses 69-75)

Before Jesus was arrested, he said to Peter, "Before the rooster crows, you will say three times that you don't know me." But Peter did not believe it. (John chapter 13 verse 38)

When the chief priests took Jesus away, Peter followed them. He waited to find out what would happen. He waited all night.

Some other people were there. They thought they had seen Peter with Jesus. They said "Are you one of Jesus's disciples?" But Peter was afraid. He said "No! I do not even know Jesus."

This happened 3 times. Then it was morning. Peter heard a rooster crow. Then he remembered what Jesus had said.

Peter felt very sad. He knew that he had let Jesus down.

(We will find out what happened next in chapter 15.)

Sometimes I let Jesus down too. Then I feel sad like Peter.

But I know Jesus forgives me when I say sorry. He does not give up on me.

Is there anything you want to say sorry to Jesus for today?

Jesus is killed

The next day was the most special day of Passover.

The Romans nailed Jesus to a big wooden cross. They left him there to die.

Jesus's disciples and his mother Mary were there. They were very sad and afraid. They thought Jesus was the saviour king. But now he was dying. Everything had gone wrong.

Jesus's body really hurt. But he asked God to forgive the people who had done this to him. Then he said "It is finished." (John chapter 19 verse 30)

After this, Jesus died.

Jesus's body was laid in a cave in a garden. This was how dead people were buried. A heavy stone was rolled in front of the cave so no one could get in.

We remember Jesus's death on Good Friday.

 Mary and the disciples saw Jesus die on the cross. How would you feel if you were there with them?

The big story...

When Jesus died, it looked like the devil had won. But this was always part of God's plan.

Jesus came to die for everyone. This was God's plan to fix the problem of sin.

So Jesus's death was not the end of the story. Jesus was about to beat the devil for good!

Sometimes things go wrong in my life. But I know God is still in charge. Nothing can stop his plans!

God has good plans for me. I know I can trust him.

Are you worried about anything? Ask God to help you trust him.

On Sunday morning, Jesus came back to life! He talked to his disciples. He told them why these things had happened. They were so happy he was alive!

Matthew chapter 28
Mark chapter 16
Luke chapter 24
John chapters 20-21

Jesus
Mary
Peter

Some women went to the cave on Sunday morning. But it was empty! Jesus's body was gone!

They saw 2 angels. The angels told them Jesus had come back to life!

Then the disciples saw Jesus alive! Other people saw him too!

Jesus helped his disciples understand why these things had happened.

Jesus is alive!

After Jesus died, his disciples were very sad.

On Sunday morning, some of the women who followed Jesus got up early. Jesus's mother Mary was with them.

The women went to the cave in the garden. They wanted to see [put spices on his body] Jesus's body. [why?]

When the women got to the cave, they saw something strange. The heavy stone had been rolled away! And the cave was empty! [when they looked inside] Jesus's body was gone!

The women were confused. They did not know what was going on.

Then 2 angels appeared! The angels told the women something wonderful. Jesus had come back to life!

> [The angels said] "This is a place to bury dead people. You should not be looking here for someone who is alive. Jesus is not here. He has become alive again!"
>
> (Luke chapter 24 verses 5-6, EASY)

The women were amazed. They ran to tell Jesus's disciples.

We remember that Jesus came back to life on Easter Sunday.

More people see Jesus

The women told Jesus's disciples what they had seen. But the disciples did not believe them. They thought it was impossible!

Later, when some of the disciples were eating together, Jesus appeared! Then they knew it was true. Jesus was alive!

2 other people who followed Jesus met a stranger on the road. The stranger asked why they were sad.

They told the stranger about Jesus. They were sad because they thought Jesus was dead.

The stranger said the saviour king had to die and come back to life. This was all part of God's plan.

Suddenly the two people knew who the stranger was. It was Jesus! Then he was gone!

Lots of other people saw Jesus alive too. He helped his disciples understand all the things that had happened. They were very happy that Jesus was alive.

What would it be like to see Jesus alive when you thought he was dead? How would you feel? What would you say?

Jesus forgives Peter

(John chapter 21 verses 1-19)

Peter was happy because Jesus was alive. But he was still sad because he had let Jesus down.

One night Peter went fishing with some of the other disciples. They kept fishing all night. But they did not catch any fish.

They saw a man on land. The man called to them. He told them to fish on the other side of the boat. When they did this, they caught lots of fish!

Then they knew the man was Jesus. Peter could not keep still. He jumped into the water. He swam to Jesus!

Jesus cooked some fish on a fire. He gave them to his disciples. Then Jesus talked to Peter. He knew what Peter had done.

Jesus said, "Peter, do you love me?" Peter said yes. Jesus asked him again, "Do you love me?" Peter said "Yes! I do!" One more time Jesus said, "Peter, do you love me?"

Peter was sad that Jesus kept asking. He said, "Yes! You know I love you." Jesus said "Look after my other disciples. And keep following me." Then Peter knew that Jesus had forgiven him.

Peter had lied about knowing Jesus 3 times. Now he had said he loved Jesus 3 times. Jesus had given Peter a new start.

When Jesus forgives me, he gives me a new start.

It does not matter what bad things I have done. If I have said sorry to Jesus, he has forgiven me. I do not have to be sad about it any more.

Jesus still loves me, just like he loved Peter. He wants me to keep following him.

Are you still sad about things you have said sorry for? Thank Jesus for giving you a new start. Ask him to how you he still loves you.

The chief priests tell a lie

The chief priests heard people saying Jesus had come back to life. They were worried. They did not know where Jesus's body had gone. But they did not want people to think Jesus was alive.

So the chief priests gave the Romans money. They told the Romans to say that Jesus's disciples had taken his body. This was not true. But lots of people believed this story.

> Why do you think the chief priests were worried? Why did they tell this lie?

The big story...

When Jesus died, it looked like the devil had won. But when he came back to life, it showed that Jesus had won! He really was the saviour king!

Death came into the world because of sin. When Jesus came back to life, it showed he was stronger than sin and death. He had beaten the devil for good.

This was a big surprise for everyone. This was not what they thought the saviour king would do. But it was God's plan all along.

Sometimes God does not do things the way I think he will. I feel confused, like Jesus's disciples.

But I know Jesus is alive. And he has beaten the devil! So I can trust that God knows what he is doing. He will make everything good in the end.

Think about what Jesus did and what happened to him. Thank Jesus for coming to save us all from sin.

 **Quick look**

God had to beat the devil to fix the problem of sin.

To beat the devil, God had to become human. Then he had to die and came back to life!

Jesus died to take away the bad things we have done and save us from sin.

Now we are forgiven and free!

When Jesus came back to life, it showed he had beaten sin, death and the devil.

Now we can have new life from God!

God's surprising plan

The Jews did not think the saviour king would die. But God knew this had to happen.

Goodness and life come from God. But people had turned away from God. Sin and death had broken the world. And people could not fix it. (Page xxx)

God had to fix the problem of sin before he could fix the world. There was only one way to do this. Sin and death come from the devil. So God had to fight the devil and win.

First God had to become human. Then he had to die and come back to life. This was how God would beat the devil, sin and death.

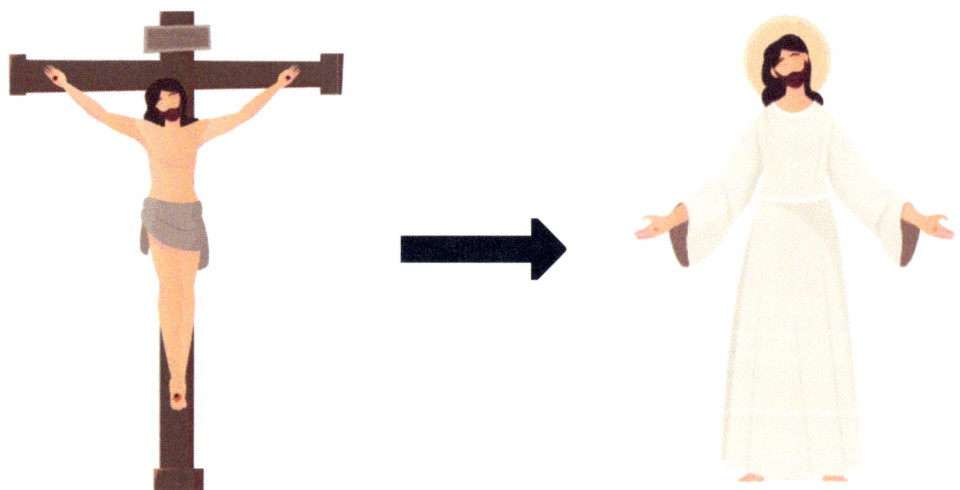

Yes, God loved the world so much that he gave his only Son, so that everyone who believes in him would not be lost but have eternal life.

(John chapter 3 verse 16, ERV)

Jesus is both God and human. He knows what it is like to be human. He knows how hard it is for us to live God's way in this broken world.

Jesus always did the right thing. But when we do bad things, he understands.

Forgiveness for sin

There are lots of ways to understand why Jesus died. One way is to think about the bad things we have done.

When Jesus died, he took away all the bad things everyone has done. Because of this, we can be forgiven.

In the past, when God's people did bad things, they had to give sin offerings to God. This was a way to say sorry to God.

In a sin offering, an animal died instead of the person. The person was forgiven. (Page xxx)

When Jesus died, he was like a sin offering for the whole world. He died instead of us. He took away all the bad things we have done. Now we can be forgiven forever!

So now, we do not have to give sin offerings to God. When we do bad things we can just say sorry to him. He forgives us because of what Jesus did.

Jesus died to take away the bad things we have done. So whatever we have done, we can still be friends with God. This was God's plan from the start!

Freedom from sin

Another way to understand why Jesus died is to think about how hard it is to do the right thing.

Sin is inside all of us. It stops us from doing what God wants. We cannot beat sin on our own. When Jesus died, he beat sin for us and set us free.

Long ago, God's people were slaves in Egypt. They could not save themselves. So God sent Moses to set them free. (Page xxx)

The Bible says all people are like slaves to sin. We cannot save ourselves. We need God to set us free.

Jesus is the only person who never did any bad things. So he is the only person strong enough to beat sin. Jesus died to beat sin and set us free.

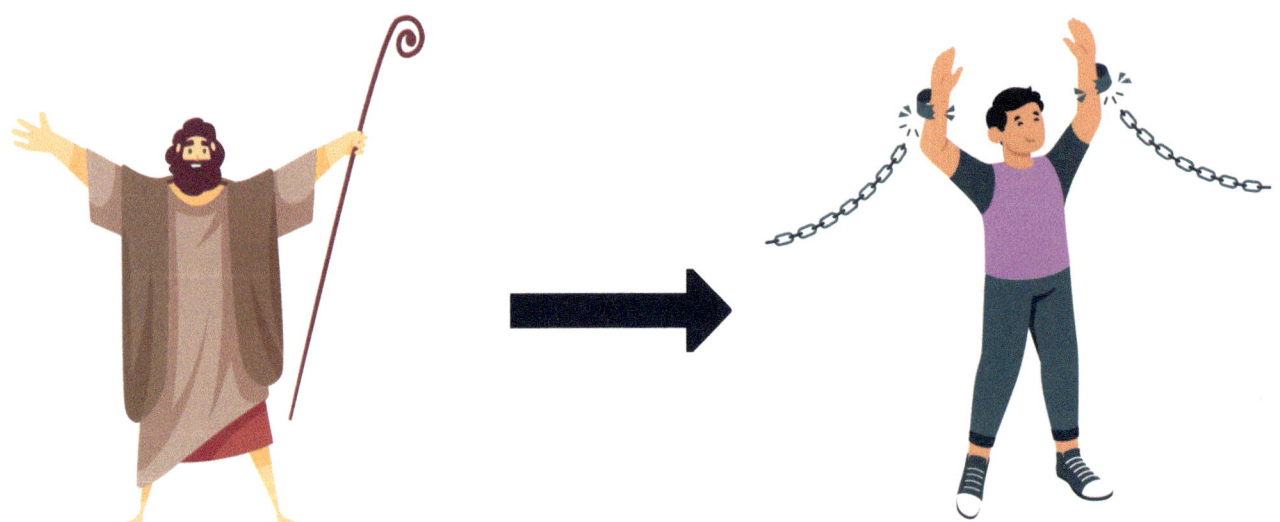

So now, we are not slaves to sin any more. We can choose to live God's way. God changes our hearts. He makes us strong. With God's help, it gets easier to do the right thing.

New life from God

Before Jesus was born, God had given Ezekiel a vision of dry bones coming back to life.

Ezekiel's vision meant that one day God would beat sin and death. He would make a way for people to come back into his goodness and life. (Page xxx)

When Jesus died, God was fighting against sin, death and the devil.

So when Jesus came back to life, it showed that God's goodness and life were stronger than sin and death. It showed that God is stronger than the devil!

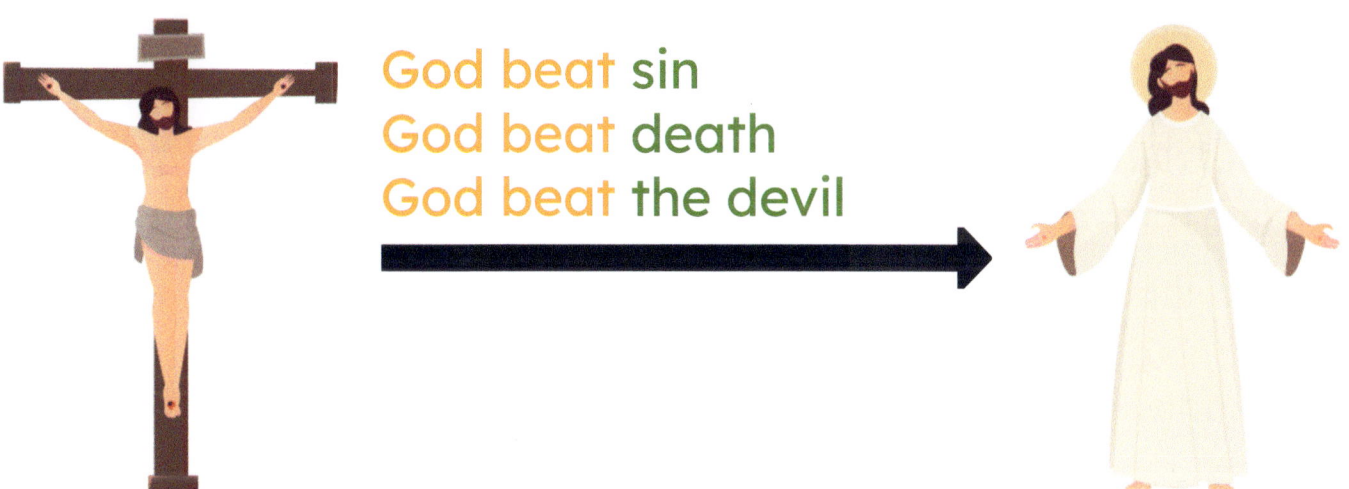

God beat sin
God beat death
God beat the devil

God has beaten sin, death and the devil. Because of this, we are forgiven and set free.

So now, we can come back into God's goodness and life! We can be friends with God and choose to live his way. And after we die, we can live forever with him.

When will God fix the world?

Jesus died to take away the bad things we have done. And he died to beat sin and set us free. He made a way for us to come back into God's goodness and life.

We could not do any of these things. Jesus did it all for us. Jesus is our saviour king. He has fixed the problem of sin!

> Jesus himself became like [people] so that, by dying, he could destroy... the devil. Jesus... died so that he could free them... He became like people so... he could bring forgiveness for the people's sins.
>
> (Hebrews chapter 2:14-15 and 17, ERV)

When God beat the devil, everything changed. God has won. The devil has lost. We know this because Jesus came back to life.

But in the world, it does not look like everything has changed. Bad things still happen. The world is not fixed yet.

One day God will end the fight. Then the devil will be gone for good. Sin and death will be gone for good. And people who trust Jesus will live forever with God. The world will be fixed forever!

But God does not want to end the fight yet. First, he wants to give everyone a chance to come back to him. He loves all the people he has made. He wants to forgive them and set them free.

In the past, God chose a special family. He wanted them to show everyone how good it was to live God's way. (Page xx)

Now, people who trust Jesus are part of this family. God wants us to tell everyone the good news about Jesus. And God wants us to show everyone how good it is to follow Jesus as our saviour king!

How can I follow Jesus?

The Bible is not just about people who lived in the past. It is also about you!

God made you and he loves you. He wants you to be his friend. He wants to show you the best way to live. And he wants to help you live that way!

Believing and doing

People who follow Jesus are called Christians. Being a Christian is about believing some things and doing some things.

→ What Christians believe

We believe that Jesus has died to save us from sin. We believe he did this because we could not save ourselves. And we believe he is alive today.

→ What Christians do

We say sorry to God for ~~our~~ all the bad things we have done. We promise to live his way. And we try to do what God wants every day.

Christians are not perfect. We still do bad things sometimes. We say sorry to God and he forgives us. And we keep trying to follow Jesus and live God's way.

Become a Christian

If you believe in Jesus and you want to live God's way, you can become a Christian today!

You can start following Jesus by telling him this is what you want to do. If you like, you can pray this prayer.

> Dear Lord Jesus,
>
> Thank you that you love me. Thank you for dying for me. Thank you for forgiving me and setting me free.
>
> I am sorry for the bad things I have done. I want to change and live God's way.
>
> Please send your Holy Spirit to live in me and help me follow you.
>
> Thank you that you are always with me.
>
> Amen.

What next?

If you have prayed this prayer, your new life with God has started! Keep talking to God and getting to know him better.

it is a good idea to tell another Christian that you have started following Jesus. They can pray for you. And they can help you if you have questions.

If you can, join a church or a Christian group. Here you can worship, pray and learn about the Bible. God wants us to meet together. That way we can all help each other.

Jesus went back to heaven. God sent his Holy Spirit to help Jesus's disciples. They told everyone about Jesus. But the leaders of the Jews tried to stop them.

Acts chapters 1-9

Jesus
Peter
Stephen
Paul (Saul)

Jesus told his disciples the Holy Spirit would come to help them.

Then Jesus went back to heaven.

The Holy Spirit came to live inside Jesus's disciples.

He helped them tell everyone about Jesus. Lots of people started following Jesus.

Followers of Jesus are called Christians.

The leaders of the Jews killed a Christian called Stephen. So most of the Christians left Jerusalem.

Saul wanted to arrest Christians. But then he became a Christian himself!

Jesus goes back to heaven

Jesus kept teaching his disciples for 40 days. Then it was time for him to go back to heaven.

Jesus told his disciples that Father God would send his Holy Spirit to help them. He told them to tell everyone about him.

> [Jesus said] "The Holy Spirit will come on you and give you power… You will tell people everywhere about me—in Jerusalem, in the rest of Judea, in Samaria, and in every part of the world."
>
> (Acts chapter 1 verse 8, ERV)

After this, Jesus's disciples saw him go up in a cloud. He was gone!

Jesus had gone back to heaven to be with Father God.

Wind and fire

10 days later, it was the festival of Pentecost. This was when the Jews remembered the laws God had given to Moses. (Page xxx) Lots of people came to Jerusalem for the festival. Some came from far away.

Jesus's disciples were all together. A strong wind came from heaven. Then the disciples saw fire resting on each other! They all started talking in languages they did not know!

This happened because of the Holy Spirit. Father God had sent his Holy Spirit to live inside the disciples and help them. This was what Jesus had promised.

The disciples went outside. The Holy Spirit made them brave. They worshipped God in different languages. Peter talked to all the people in a loud voice. He told them about Jesus.

The people heard the disciples talking in their own languages. They were amazed! Lots of them believed what Peter said. They joined the disciples and started to follow Jesus.

 How did the Holy Spirit help the disciples? How were they different after the Holy Spirit came?

Stephen is killed

More and more people started following Jesus. People who follow Jesus are called Christians.

The Christians told everyone that Jesus had come back to life. The Holy Spirit gave them power to heal people, just like Jesus did!

But all this made the leaders of the Jews angry. They tried to stop the Christians talking about Jesus.

One of the Christians was called Stephen. Some people told the leaders that Stephen was causing trouble. The leaders arrested him.

Stephen told the leaders of the Jews about Jesus. He said they had killed the saviour king! This made the leaders very angry. They took Stephen outside Jerusalem. They threw stones at him until he died.

Before he died, Stephen prayed to Jesus. He asked Jesus to forgive the people who killed him.

A man called Saul watched this happen. Saul did not believe what Stephen said about Jesus. He thought it was a good thing that Stephen was killed. (Later, Saul was called Paul.)

After Stephen died, Jerusalem was not safe for Christians. Saul and the leaders of the Jews were trying to put them in prison. Most of the Christians left Jerusalem. Only Jesus's disciples stayed.

Saul becomes a Christian

(Acts chapter 9 verses 1-31)

Saul was going to a town called Damascus. He was looking for Christians. He wanted to arrest them.

On the way, something strange happened. A light appeared from heaven. Saul heard a voice say, "Saul! Why do you fight against me?" (Acts chapter 9 verse 4, EASY)

Saul was afraid. He said, "Lord, who are you?" The voice said, "I am Jesus. And you are fighting against me." (Acts chapter 9 verse 5, EASY) Jesus said someone in Damascus would tell Saul what to do next.

When the light was gone, Saul was blind! He went into Damascus. He stayed there and waited.

God told a man called Ananias to talk to Saul. Ananias was a Christian. He knew all about Saul. He was afraid that Saul would arrest him. But he did what God said.

Ananias told Saul what God had said. He put his hands on Saul's eyes. Something fell out of Saul's eyes. Then he could see again!

Now Saul believed in Jesus. He became a Christian. His whole life changed. Saul started telling everyone about Jesus!

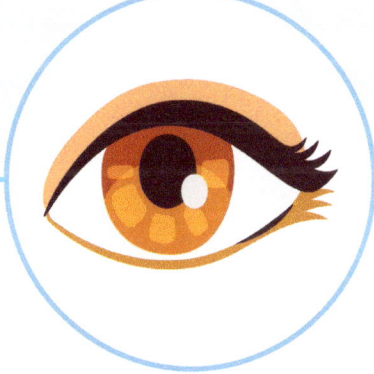

How do you think Saul's life changed after he became a Christian? Has following Jesus changed anything in your life?

Jesus died for everyone. He wants everyone to be friends with God.

Jesus even loves people who do bad things. He wants to help them change, like Paul. Saul

Think about someone you know who is not a Christian. Ask Jesus to show them who he is and how much he loves them.

The big story...

Long ago, God had made a promise to Ezekiel. (Page xxx) God said one day his Holy Spirit would live inside people. Now that promise had come true!

The Holy Spirit lives inside Christians. He helps us to live God's way. He changes our hearts. He makes us more like Jesus.

The Holy Spirit can help me too. He wants to change my heart and help me follow Jesus.

If you are a Christian, thank the Holy Spirit for living inside you and helping you.

If you are not a Christian, think about whether you would like to start following Jesus, like ~~Paul~~ did.

Saul

God told Peter that people everywhere could follow Jesus. Saul changed his name to Paul, and told people in lots of places about Jesus.

Acts chapters 10-28

Paul (Saul)
Barnabas
Peter

from this point shouldn't you call saul PAUL? This is the overview!

Barnabas told the other Christians that Saul had changed. They let Saul join them.

God told Peter that people who were not Jews could follow Jesus too.

Saul changed his name to Paul. He went to lots of places. He told everyone about Jesus and started lots of churches.

Paul was put in prison. But he kept following Jesus. He wrote letters to the churches.

It was not safe to follow Jesus. But the Christians did not give up.

Saul joins the Christians

The Christians were still afraid of Saul. They did not believe Saul had really changed.

One of the Christians was called Barnabas. He helped Saul. He told the others that Saul had heard Jesus's voice.

Saul really was a follower of Jesus! The others believed Barnabas. They let Saul join them.

 Saul had done bad things to Christians, but now he was a Christian himself! How do you think the other Christians felt about this?

What might have helped the other Christians to forgive Saul and be friends with him?

Peter has a vision

(Acts chapter 10)

So far, all the Christians were Jews, from Abraham's family. God had chosen this family long ago. (Page xxx) If someone wanted to join God's people, they had to become a Jew.

A Roman called Cornelius lived in Jerusalem. He was not a Jew. But he wanted to know about God. An angel talked to Cornelius in a vision. The angel told him to talk to Peter. So Cornelius sent some men to find Peter.

The next day, Peter was praying. God showed him a vision too. In Peter's vision, God told him to eat some meat. But the meat was from animals the Jews did not eat. God's laws said these animals were unclean.

Peter said "I will not eat this. It is unclean." Then God said, "I have made it clean." This happened 3 times.

Then Cornelius's men came. They told Peter about Cornelius's vision. Now Peter knew what his vision meant. God was telling Peter that something important had changed.

Jesus had died for everyone's sin. So now everyone could join God's family! Even people who were not Jews could follow Jesus!

This made Cornelius very happy. He became a Christian that day!

Peter began to speak: "I really understand now that God does not consider some people to be better than others. He accepts anyone who worships him and does what is right. It is not important what nation they come from."

(Acts chapter 10 verses 34-35 ERV)

Cornelius was the first Christian from outside Abraham's family. But today there are Christians all over the world!

It does not matter where I come from. God made me and he loves me. God made everyone! And he loves everyone the same.

Talk to God about some of the people you know. Thank God that he loves them all. Ask him to do good things for them.

Jesus is for everyone!

God gave Saul a special job to do. He told Saul to go to lots of places and tell everyone about Jesus.

The places Saul went are now in Turkey, Italy and Greece. These places were all ruled by the Romans. So Saul changed his name to a Roman name. His new name was Paul.

Everywhere Paul went, he told people about Jesus. Some people Paul met were Jews. Paul told them Jesus was their saviour king.

Other people were not Jews. They worshipped other gods. Paul told them about the real God. He said God really loved them. Because of Jesus, they could join God's family!

Lots of people became Christians. Paul baptised them by dipping them in water. This was a sign that they had started a new life following Jesus. Christians are still baptised today.

Paul took Barnabas and other helpers with him. In each place, they started a church. These were not buildings. They were groups of Christians who met in each other's houses. They worshipped God and learned about Jesus together.

 Are you part of a church? What are some good things about being part of a church?

Paul in prison

The leaders of the Jews and the Romans did not like what Paul was doing. They put him in prison.

Even in prison, Paul kept following Jesus. He could not visit the churches, so he wrote letters to them instead.

Do you need to say this happened in Rome?

Lots of Christians were killed for telling people about Jesus. In the end, Paul was probably killed too.

It was not safe to follow Jesus. But the Holy Spirit made the Christians brave. They did not give up. They knew God wanted everyone to know the good news about Jesus.

The big story...

Long ago, God had promised to do good things for the whole world because of Abraham's family. (Page xxx)

Now that promise had come true! Jesus had died for the whole world. Now people everywhere can follow Jesus and be friends with God. This is a wonderful thing!

Sometimes following Jesus can be hard. Other people might not understand. They might make fun of me.

in the world

And there are still some places where it is not safe to follow Jesus. Christians are still put in prison and killed.

But the Holy Spirit makes us brave. He helps us to keep going and not give up.

Is following Jesus ever hard for you? Ask the Holy Spirit to help you not to give up.

Pray for Christians in places that are not safe. Ask the Holy Spirit to help them not to give up.

 **Quick look**

God has shown himself to us in 3 different ways: Father, Son and Holy Spirit.

God is called 'The Trinity.'

Father God made us and loves us.

Jesus (God's son) died for us.

The Holy Spirit lives inside Christians and helps us.

The Holy Spirit grows good fruit in us. And he gives us good gifts.

God is more amazing than we can understand.

Father, Son and Holy Spirit

Christians believe there is only one God. But God has shown himself to us in 3 different ways.

First, God showed himself as Father God.

Then God showed himself as Jesus. Sometimes Jesus is called God's Son.

Last, God showed himself as the Holy Spirit.

Father God

Jesus
(God's Son)

Holy Spirit

So God is Father, Son and Holy Spirit. This is why we call God 'The Trinity', which means '3 in 1'.

But the Father, Son and Holy Spirit are not different people. They are joined together as one God.

[Jesus said,] "Make followers of all people in the world. Baptise them in the name of the Father and the Son and the Holy Spirit."

(Matthew chapter 28 verse 19, ERV)

Working Together

Father God, Jesus and the Holy Spirit are joined together as one God. They always agree. They work in different ways. But they are always working together.

→ Father God

Father God is in heaven. He made us and he loves us.

He sent Jesus to fix the problem of sin. Then he sent the Holy Spirit to help Christians.

→ Jesus

At the start, Jesus was in heaven with Father God. Then he became human and lived in the world.

Jesus is human and God. He died for our sin and came back to life. Then he went back to heaven.

→ The Holy Spirit

The Holy Spirit works in the world. After Jesus went back to heaven, the Holy Spirit came to live inside Christians.

The Holy Spirit helps us live God's way. Sometimes we picture him as a dove. (Page xxx)

God's special home

In the past, the Temple was God's special home. It was where he lived with his people. (Page xxx)

But now, Christians are God's special home. In one of his letters, Paul said, 'Your body is a temple for the Holy Spirit… that lives in you.' (1 Corinthians chapter 6 verse 19, ERV)

When we start to follow Jesus, the Holy Spirit comes to live inside us. He helps us live God's way. He changes our hearts and makes us more like Jesus.

How the Holy Spirit helps us

The Holy Spirit helps us in 2 big ways. He grows good fruit in us. And he gives us good gifts.

→ Fruit from the Holy Spirit

Long ago, God said his people were like a vineyard of fruit trees. He wanted them to grow good fruit, like kindness. (Page xxx)

We could not grow this good fruit because of sin. But now the Holy Spirit grows good fruit in us. This is how the Holy Spirit makes us more like Jesus.

In one of his letters, Paul said the fruit of the Holy Spirit is 'love, joy, peace, patience, kindness, goodness, faithfulness, gentleness and self-control.' (Galatians chapter 5 verse 22, ERV)

→ Gifts from the Holy Spirit

The Holy Spirit also gives us good gifts. He makes some people good at teaching or helping people who are sad. Some people have special wisdom. Others can make sick people better like Jesus did.

There are lots of other gifts too. (1 Corinthians chapter 12 verses 7-10 and Romans chapter 12 verses 6-8)

We all have different gifts from the Holy Spirit. We can use our gifts to help each other and work with God to make the world better.

God is amazing!

Thinking about the Trinity can be confusing. It reminds us that God is very different from us.

God is bigger and stronger than us. He sees everything and knows everything. God is more amazing than we can ever understand.

It is amazing to know that Father God made us and wants us to be his friends.

It is amazing to know that Jesus became a man and died for us.

And it is amazing to know that the Holy Spirit lives inside us and helps us every day.

God loves us and helps us in so many different ways. That really is amazing!

Paul and other Christians wrote letters. They wrote about what Christians believe and how God wants Christians to live.

Romans
1 and 2 Corinthians
Galatians
Ephesians
Philippians
Colossians
1 and 2 Thessalonians
1 and 2 Timothy

Titus
Philemon
Hebrews
James
1 and 2 Peter
1, 2 and 3 John
Jude

Paul
Peter
John
Timothy
Titus
Philemon

There are **21** letters in the Bible.

They teach us more about Jesus. They teach us how to live as Christians.

Paul, Peter, John and others wrote letters to churches.

Paul wrote letters to his friends too.

In the past God gave his people laws. Now he gives us grace.

Now we only need to trust Jesus and follow him. This is a new way to be friends with God.

God wants Christians to love each other and work together.

We can help each other follow Jesus.

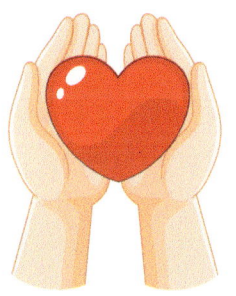

Sending Letters

Lots of people had started to follow Jesus. There were new Christians and new churches in lots of different places.

But these Christians did not understand everything yet. They needed help to learn more about Jesus and how to live God's way.

Paul and other Christians visited the churches when they could. And they wrote letters too.

Each letter was written on scroll. Someone had to take it to the person or people it was for.

Some letters were just for one person. Other letters were passed around different churches so more people could read them.

We can read 21 of those letters in the Bible.

Letters to churches and friends

Letters to churches

 Paul wrote letters to the churches he started. Peter, John and others wrote letters to churches too.

The letters told the churches more about Jesus and how to live as Christians. And sometimes the letters told them about things they were doing wrong.

Some churches wrote to Paul to ask questions. Their letters are not in the Bible. But Paul answered their questions in his letters to them.

Letters to friends

 Paul also wrote letters to his friends.

Paul wrote to Timothy and Titus. They were church leaders. Paul helped them fix problems in their churches. He told them how to lead their churches well.

Paul wrote to Philemon. Philemon's slave had run away. Then the slave had met Paul and become a Christian!

Paul sent the slave back to Philemon with a letter. Paul told Philemon that he and his slave were now like brothers because they were both Christians.

Paul writes a letter from prison

(Philippians chapter 1 verses 12-26, chapter 2 verses 25-28, and chapter 4 verses 14-19)

Paul was in prison. Prisoners had to buy their own food. But Paul did not have much money.

Paul had started a church in a town called Philippi. The Christians there wanted to help Paul. They sent a man called Epaphroditus to give some money to Paul.

Epaphroditus had to go a long way. He stayed with Paul for some time. Then Paul asked Epaphroditus to take a letter back to the church in Philippi.

In his letter, Paul said he was still telling people about Jesus. He wanted to do whatever God told him. He did not mind if he was in prison, or even if he stayed alive.

Paul knew that whatever happened, God was with him. And he knew that after he died he would be with God forever.

Paul said, "Christ is the one who gives me the strength I need to do whatever I must do." (Philippians chapter 4 verse 13, ERV)

Epaphroditus took Paul's letter back to the church in Philippi. Most people could not read. So someone read the letter to the whole church. The Christians were happy to hear from Paul.

Now that I know Christ Jesus as my Lord, that is the most valuable thing. Nothing else is important at all. I have thrown everything else away, so that I can serve Christ. All those other things are like dirt to me. I think about them like that, so that I can have Christ.

(Philippians chapter 3 verse 8, EASY)

Paul's letter helped the Christians in Philippi. They knew Paul kept following Jesus even when it was hard.

This helped the Christians keep following Jesus even when it was hard. They knew God was with them, like he was with Paul.

Other Christians help me follow Jesus too. They help me keep going when it is hard.

Can you think of someone who helps you to keep following Jesus? Thank to God for them now. Maybe you could say 'Thank you' to them too!

God's gift of grace

In the past, God gave his people laws. People had to keep God's laws. This was the way to be friends with God. (Page xxx)

God's laws helped his people understand how to live God's way. But they could not do it. They could not beat sin on their own.

That is why Jesus came. Jesus kept all God's laws and always lived God's way. Then he died to beat sin, death, and the devil. (Page xxx)

Jesus did all this for us. He did the things we could not do. He made a new way for us to be friends with God.

Now, we do not have to keep laws to be friends with God. We only need to trust Jesus and follow him as our saviour king.

This is called grace. It is a free gift from God.

Grace does not mean we stop living God's way. Grace means we can live God's way better than before!

We do not have to worry about sin any more. We know we are forgiven and free! So now, we want to live God's way because we love him and trust him. The Holy Spirit lives inside us and helps us.

> Which do you think is better, laws or grace? Why?
>
> How does it feel to know that you do not have to keep laws to be God's friend?

Living as a Christian

The letters teach us 3 important things about how to live as a Christian.

→ Love each other

Christians should love each other. This means being kind and helping each other.

It means saying sorry when we hurt someone too. And it means forgiving people when they hurt us.

→ Follow Jesus

Christians should stay close to Jesus. We should do what Jesus said and try to be like him. This is how to live God's way. We do this because we love God. We want to make him happy.

When we do bad things, we say sorry to God and start again. He always forgives us.

As we follow Jesus, the Holy Spirit changes our hearts. He shows us what God wants. He grows good fruit in us to make us more like Jesus.

→ Keep trusting God

Christians should keep trusting God, even when life is hard. God is always with us, and he helps us.

One day God will fix the world. Then everything will be good forever.

Life in church

The letters teach us 2 important things about what life in church should be like.

→ Everyone is important

Christians are like a body that has lots of different parts. God has made us all different. This means we can all help each other follow Jesus.

God says we are all important. So we should not think some Christians are better than others. God wants us all to work together and show people what he is like.
(1 Corinthians chapter 12 verses 12-27)

We meet in churches where we live. But all the Christians in the world together are one big church. Paul said we are like Jesus's body, doing the things he wants us to do.

→ We need good leaders

Church leaders should be kind and help others. They should not think they are more important than everyone else. They should not bully people or tell lies.

Church leaders should know the Bible well. They should teach what the Bible says. (Titus chapter 1 verses 6-9)

 Think about the Christians you know. How are they different? How do they help you follow Jesus?

How do you help other Christians follow Jesus? If you do not know, you can ask them!

212

The big story...

Before he went to heaven, Jesus promised he would come back one day. Then he would make everything good.

The new Christians trusted this promise. They met in churches. The Holy Spirit made them more like Jesus. And they kept going, even when life was hard.

God makes us all different. He does not want me to be the same as everyone else.

But God does want us all to be loving, patient and kind. This is what Jesus was like. And it is the fruit the Holy Spirit grows in us. This is good for us, and for the whole world.

If you are a Christian, ask the Holy Spirit to show you what good fruit he is growing in you. Ask him to keep making you more like Jesus.

God gave a vision to John. John saw that Jesus will come back one day. Then God will make everything good forever. We are still waiting for this to happen.

Revelation

John
Jesus

216

God gave a vision to a man called John.

The vision gave the Christians hope.

John saw God as king in heaven. Then he saw Jesus as a lamb.

John saw the devil as a dragon. The devil was making trouble in the world.

John saw Jesus winning a war. Then he saw God set everything right.

John saw God make everything good. Now the whole world was God's kingdom.

One day this will happen. Then we will see that God really has fixed the world! We will live forever with him.

An amazing vision

It was not safe to be a Christian. Lots of Jesus's followers were put in prison or killed. A Christian leader called John was sent to live on an island far away from his home.

One day, God showed John an amazing vision. God told John to write the vision down and send it to 7 churches in different places.

John's vision was about what was happening at the time, and what would happen in the future.

The things John saw in his vision were very strange. John talked about them in word-pictures. Some were like the pictures God gave the prophets long ago.

God gave John this vision to give the Christians hope. It helped them keep following Jesus when life was hard.

Messages for 7 churches

(Revelation chapters 1-3)

At the start of John's vision, Jesus gave him messages for 7 churches. Jesus said the churches were like lights. They were meant to show Jesus to the world.

In his messages, Jesus told the churches what they were doing well. And he told them where they were going wrong.

Some churches had started to turn away from God. Some were listening to bad teachers who told them to do bad things *that were not right.* One church did not love Jesus like they used to.

Jesus told these churches to say sorry and come back to God.

Some churches were going through hard times. They were poor and did not feel strong. People were trying to shut them down.

Jesus told these churches not to be afraid. If they kept going, one day they would live with God forever.

Some churches were still trusting God. They were still living God's way, even when it was hard.

Jesus was very pleased with these churches. He promised God would give them wonderful things in the future. No one would take these things away from them.

219

Jesus wanted the 7 churches to show him to the world. He wants me to show him to the world too.

I can do this by following Jesus and telling people what he has done for me.

Ask Jesus to show you what you are doing well and where you are going wrong. Ask the Holy Spirit to help you show Jesus to the world.

A picture of heaven

John saw God as the king on a throne. Then he saw Jesus. But Jesus looked like a lamb who had been killed and come back to life!

The meaning of this picture was very special. In the past, God's people had killed lambs as sin offerings. But now, Jesus had died as a sin offering for the whole world. (Page xxx) Jesus was like those lambs, but better.

This picture reminded the Christians that Jesus had taken away the bad things they had done. He had died and come back to life. Now Jesus was alive with God in heaven.

Can you remember some other word-pictures of Jesus in the Bible?

If you like, draw a picture that reminds you what Jesus means to you.

Trouble in the world

After this, John saw some bad things. (in his vision) He saw war, illness and death in the world. He saw Christians who had been killed.

Then John saw a dragon and 2 strange animals. They made trouble for Christians in the world.

The dragon was a picture of the devil. The animals were pictures of powerful people who hate God.

These pictures meant that things in the world would be hard in the world for a long time.

God fixes the world

Next, John saw a big fight. He saw Jesus riding on a white horse. John saw all the bad things end. He saw God throw the dragon into fire. Then the dragon was gone. God had ended the fight!

Then John saw all the people who ever lived. He saw God as the good judge who sets things right. God looked at the things each person had done. He decided what should happen to them.

John saw some people put in the lake of fire. But the people who trusted Jesus lived with God forever.

At the end of his vision, John saw something wonderful. He saw a beautiful city coming down from heaven. It was a new Jerusalem where God would be king.

Now the whole world was God's kingdom. All bad things were gone. God had fixed the world and made everything good forever.

> I heard a loud voice from the throne. It said, "Now God's home is with people… There will be no more death, sadness, crying, or pain. All the old ways are gone." The one who was sitting on the throne said, "Look, I am making everything new!"
>
> (Revelation chapter 21 verses 3-5, ERV)

Waiting for God's kingdom

John's vision is very hard to understand. Christians do not all agree about what it means, or how these things will happen.

But here are some things we do know.

→ God is the king over everything

Bad things will keep happening in the world. But God is still the king. We can still trust that he will keep his promises.

→ Jesus will come back with power

When Jesus comes back, everyone will know he is God.

→ God is the good judge who sets things right

God will decide what happens to each person. We do not know everything about this. But we know God is good, and he loves people. We can trust him to make things right.

→ God will fix the world

When God ends the fight, the devil and all bad things will be gone. The world will not be broken any more. Everything will be good.

→ Christians will live forever in God's kingdom

Christians have been saved by Jesus. The bad things we have done are forgiven. God promises that we will live forever with him.

We are still waiting for these things to happen. So John's vision gives us hope. It helps us keep following Jesus when life is hard.

 What will it be like when the whole world is God's kingdom? What will be the same? What will be different?

God has kept lots of promises. So I can trust that he will keep these promises too.

By following Jesus, I help God bring his kingdom into the world. And I can look forward to the day when the whole world will be God's kingdom. He will set everything right. He will make everything good forever.

Talk to God about some ways you could make the world better. Ask him to help you do something good today.

The big story...

We know the devil is beaten. But he is still making trouble in the world. God's plan is not finished yet.

We are waiting for Jesus to come back. Then God will fix the world. The devil and all bad things will be gone. The whole world will be God's kingdom. And we will live forever with him.

The Bible ends with this prayer. (Revelation chapter 22 verses 20-21)

> Jesus says, "I am coming soon."
> Yes. Come, Lord Jesus!
> May the grace of the Lord Jesus
> be with God's people.
> Amen.

Is this the end?

This is the end of the big story of the Bible. But God's big story goes on forever.

You can have your own story with God too!

Your story with God is your friendship with him and the good things you do together.

It will have some ups and downs. Sometimes it will be hard. And sometimes it will be wonderful.

Keep following Jesus, and have fun!

About Jo + Read More

Thanks

229

Index of people

* We do not know if these 2 Johns are the same person or different people.

230

Index of books

Genesis - Chapters 1, 2, 3

Exodus
Leviticus
Numbers
Deuteronomy
— 4 z

Joshua
Judges
Ruth
— 5

1 Samuel 5 6

2 Samuel 6

1 Kings 6 8

2 Kings 8

1 Chronicles 6

2 Chronicles 6 8

Ezra
Nehemiah
Esther
— 11

Job
Psalms
Proverbs
Ecclesiastes
Song of Songs
— 7

Isaiah 9

Jeremiah 9 10

Lamentations
Ezekiel
Daniel
— 10

Hosea
Joel
Amos
Obadiah
Jonah
Micah
Nahum
Habakkuk
Zephaniah
— 9

Haggai
Zechariah
Malachi
— 11

Matthew
Mark
Luke
John
— 12 13 z 14 15

Acts 16 17

Romans
1 and 2 Corinthians
Galatians
Ephesians
Philippians
Colossians
1 and 2 Thessalonians
1 and 2 Timothy
Titus
Philemon
Hebrews
James
1 and 2 Peter
1,2 and 3 John
Jude
— 18

Revelation 19

231

Word meanings

232

BV - #0070 - 250425 - C231 - 279/216/13 - WB - 9781739927332 - Matt Lamination